How to
EXPORT

How to EXPORT

WITH A FOREWORD BY
SIR JAMES CLEMINSON

A
Daily Telegraph
BUSINESS ENTERPRISE BOOK

Published by Telegraph Publications
Peterborough Court, At South Quay,
181 Marsh Wall, London E14 9SR

© The Daily Telegraph/William Curtis Ltd 1988

This book is sold subject to the condition that it shall not, by way of trade or otherwise, be lent, re-sold, hired out or otherwise circulated without the publisher's prior consent in any form of binding or cover other than that in which it is published.

All rights reserved. No part of this work may be reproduced or transmitted by any means without permission.

Whilst every care has been taken to ensure the accuracy of the contents of this work, no responsibility for loss occasioned to any person acting or refraining from action as a result of any statement in it can be accepted by the publisher.

Designed and Typeset by Litho Link Ltd, Welshpool, Wales
Printed in Great Britain by Biddles Ltd, Guildford

British Library Cataloguing in Publication Data

How to export
1. Export marketing 2. Small business 658.8'48 HF1009.5
ISBN 0-86367-200-0

THE CONTRIBUTORS

We would like to express our appreciation of the help given by the following contributors in the preparation of this book.

Roy Humphries
Bain Clarkson Ltd., International Insurance Brokers

B W Gould
Birmingham Chamber of Industry & Commerce

British Overseas Trade Board (BOTB)

J R Wilson
Director-General, Institute of Export

J F White
Commercial Director, Institute of Freight Forwarders

David R Young
International Banking Division, National Westminster Bank PLC

Charles Freebury
Director, Simplification of International Trade Procedures Board (SITPRO)

Contents

Foreword 9

Introduction 13

1 Testing the Market – Finding Out 17
Where to find information and advice 17
Carrying out market research 18

2 Factors to be Considered Before Deciding to Export 29
 29
How will existing resources be affected? 32
What additional resources will be needed? 36
Keeping in touch

3 To Which Countries Should I Export? 39
Access 40
Language and culture 41
Tariffs and trade blocs 41
Payment 43

4 Opening Up Export Markets 47
What kind of sales organisation? 47
Arranging field visits 51
Channels of communication 52
Advice and assistance 53

5 Getting Paid 57
Payment in advance 58
The Documentary Letter of Credit 59
Documentary collection 64

	Open account	65
	Which currency?	66
	Arranging finance	68

6 Cargo Insurance — **71**
   Your liabilities — 71
   The carrier's liabilities — 73
   Making a claim — 75

7 Methods of Transport — **77**
   Air — 78
   Road — 79
   Rail — 81
   Sea — 81
   Freight forwarders — 84

8 Documentation — **85**
   What forms will you normally have to supply? — 86
   Other forms — 88
   Single Administrative Document — 89

9 Case Studies — **91**

Appendices
   I: Samples of commonly used documents — 97
   II: Exporter's checklist — 125
   III: Glossary of commonly used export conditions of sale — 127
   IV: List of useful names and addresses — 129
   V: Seaports in the UK — 135
   VI: Inland clearance depots, Inland rail depots and Free zones — 139
   VII: World currencies — 141

Index — **153**

Foreword

So why should you want to export at all? Certainly there were times during my 40 years in exporting when I wondered whether it was worth the heartache.

Many companies which already export will say that they saw a market potential for their product or service overseas. Of course, it is a fundamental requirement that there should be a demand for what you produce. In itself, this should not be the sole reason for taking the plunge, particularly when it is not as straightforward selling in overseas markets as it is at home.

Having gauged the potential market overseas for your product, the question you must then ask is: 'What is in it for my business?' And perhaps the most compelling answer is that it could mean an increase in your revenue and your profits. Indeed, since becoming Chairman of the British Overseas Trade Board (BOTB) in July 1986, I have met more than one now thriving company who were on the verge of going out of business before – almost in desperation – seeking a market for their products overseas. Now I do not think I should suggest that more British companies allow themselves to teeter on the brink of bankruptcy before venturing from these shores. But it does show what exporting can do.

Of course, there are ways other than improving profitability in which exporting can be good for your business. Exporting helps spread your business risks – you are not relying on just one market, which can leave you very vulnerable to fluctuations in its economy. Selling in overseas markets also helps your products keep their competitive edge and puts you in a better position to keep an eye on your overseas competitors. For Britain is an open market and it is likely your main international competitors are here too.

Not least, increased sales from exporting will probably mean increased production and that could lead to the creation of more jobs.

Smaller firms could be forgiven for thinking that exporting is just for their big cousins who have the resources for running a dedicated in-house export department. Nothing could be further from the truth. It is an assumption that in many cases stems from ignorance and a lack of information which, I am sure, this book will help to overcome.

Exporting certainly is not easy; but all too often the difficulties are overestimated by those who have never tried. Indeed, many small companies which are successful exporters will tell you that as you gain greater experience and confidence, many initial problems can be overcome with comparative ease.

The purpose of this book is to give you some idea of what is involved, to tell you the sort of questions you should ask and who will be able to give you the right answers. It does *not* set out to be a complete 'do it yourself export handbook' which will turn you into an instant expert. No book can accomplish that. For it is only from the experience gained by actually going out into the world's markets and selling that expertise will be built up.

The important thing to remember is that you do not have to go into exporting all alone. It would be foolish to try. Exporting is not just a question of popping on an aeroplane with a suitcase of samples. You will almost certainly return home having sold nothing and swearing that you will never try to export again.

Follow the guidance and advice contained in this book and take advantage of the help on offer from the many organisations mentioned and you should be able to avoid the pitfalls that can await the unwary as they take their first steps into exporting. It is vital that you make sure the groundwork is done before you even think about buying your airline tickets.

Many a small company asking the question: 'Where do I start?' has found the answer by simply making contact with their local regional office of the British Overseas Trade Board – the telephone number of which can be found in Appendix IV of this book and, of course, in *Yellow Pages* under 'Export Consultants'. The BOTB's services include help with initial market research, with visiting a chosen market and with establishing yourself in that market. There are many other

Foreword

ways in which the BOTB can help you get started or, if you are already exporting, to expand into new markets.

There is a host of other organisations that will help you – your local chamber of commerce, your own trade association and perhaps there is an export club in your area. Quite apart from the help they can provide, you will also have the opportunity of meeting and talking to other businessmen who are already exporters – a great deal can be learned from their experience. Other bodies, such as the Institute of Export and your own bank, are all able to provide sound professional advice and assistance.

By making contact with such organisations, you will also hear about the many conferences and seminars which take place throughout the United Kingdom. Some deal with various aspects of exporting and the skills required, while others provide information about specific markets and sectors where there are good sales opportunities – perhaps for your product.

However, the most important ingredient for successful exporting is commitment. Exporting needs to be an integral part of your business strategy – not just something to be dropped or picked up as the home market rises and falls. Be prepared to invest time and money and do not expect an immediate and spectacular return. It can happen, but for most companies exporting is a long-term investment.

Perhaps a measure of the potential rewards can be gauged from some research carried out on behalf of the BOTB's Small Firms Committee. They were looking at manufacturing companies in the £1 million to £10 million turnover bracket. Out of some 12,000 UK companies in this bracket, only half were found to be exporters at all. Of those 6,000, only 2,000 were what could be termed committed or active exporters and they accounted for some 80 per cent of the total – some £4.4 billion-worth of exports a year. The other 4,000 were passive in that they tended to export only occasionally in response to an order that happened to come their way.

What would be the effect if those 4,000 passive exporters were to match the performance of their active counterparts? Britain's exports would be boosted by an incredible £5.2 billion a year – well over £0.5 million of British goods every *hour*. That is without the non-exporting 6,000. Surely many of them must have something to sell overseas if they can sell here in the UK.

How to Export

It is a challenge, but it all adds up to exporting being big business even for small firms. And there could not be a better time with more favourable conditions for British firms to take up this challenge. Exchange rates are to our advantage. In many markets we have low inflation and our goods are not only competitive in terms of cost but in quality as well.

I hope your reading of this book will be the first step towards boosting your profits through exporting.

Sir James Cleminson
Chairman
The British Overseas Trade Board

Introduction

In his essay *Thoughts on Commercial Subjects*, Benjamin Franklin (1706-1790) said 'No nation was ever ruined by trade'. The same statement is equally valid today when applied to companies. However, before making the decision to export, consider carefully why you need to do so. There is only one good reason for exporting and that is for profit. Exporting should not be considered as an easy option because your business in the UK is not doing so well. Costly and possibly fatal mistakes can be made in the overseas market. Exporting is merely one option available when seeking to rectify this problem.

Do not be put off by the fallacy that only large companies export abroad and succeed. Indeed, the small business, over the last decade, has come into its own as it is able to offer speedy decisions, flexibility, specialised products and personalised service, all of which are appreciated in the international market place.

Pitfalls can be found in any area of trade, and to minimise this risk you need to ask yourself the right commercial questions and have the right answers before you make the move into exporting. This book goes through the process in a logical sequence, telling you what questions should be asked, what commercial avenues explored, and finally when the decision to export has been made how actually to do it. The mystique which surrounds exporting has been dispelled by the experts who have contributed to this title, thus producing an easily understood and highly workable guide.

One of the first questions you need to ask yourself is 'Do I need to export at all?' If your home market share is static then exporting is just one option available. Rather you should ask yourself the following questions:

'Do I have excess capacity (both in human resources and product)?'

'Do I have a saleable product for overseas buyers?'

'Will I be able to cover all my expenses and make a profit for my business?'

Before answering these questions take a step back and examine your company's affairs closely to see whether or not you have the spare capacity. Look not only for surplus capacity in production but also at the human resources side too. If either one or both do not stand up to examination then proceed no further until they have been rectified. If you do go ahead regardless and are successful in selling to an overseas market, then should production not meet demand or your staff be unable to cope you will lose orders and worse still, spoil your future chances. Remember you and/or your staff should be familiar with (a) the language of the country to which you are exporting (b) the shipping procedures and (c) the product itself.

Next, take a closer look at your product and at the country or countries to which you are seeking to export. Is there market there for your product? If not, is your product adaptable and will the hybrid be saleable? Packaging plays an important role here; it has been known for a product which was being sold overseas and doing very well for sales to slump suddenly when the packaging was altered. Research revealed that it was the packaging which actually sold the product and not the product itself.

Have you analysed how much it will cost to export your product, including manufacture, marketing, skilled staff, shipping, and so on? The one thing you can rely on is that it is going to cost you money. From researching the potential market place right through to shipping the product, you will have to find the necessary finance to make it work. And be warned, do not undercapitalise your venture. When working out your budget, take a leaf out of the competitions' books, they plan their budgets not for one year but for at least three years ahead, as they know that it can take that length of time to get the business 'off the ground'.

Once you have got the right answers assembled and your research indicates potential, then ask yourself 'Am I (and my

Introduction

workforce) committed to exporting?' 'Are my resources such that one person can be solely committed to monitoring the work through, dealing with the problems, actioning and getting results?' Only you will be able to answer those questions and know whether or not your company is in a position to go ahead.

What can be exported?

There are three main commodity areas for export: product, service and know-how. The easiest of these to export is 'know-how'. It needs no shipping, does not need to be manufactured, and the size of organisation can be smaller. However, you need to ensure that the legal details are absolutely correct and that you have 'licensed' your 'know-how'. Service is the next easiest area to export, followed finally by product.

Selling overseas is an attractive proposition; it does spread your risks in the different world economies. But if our home economy is not doing so well then chances are that the foreign one might not be doing so well either.

Cost your product carefully. Not only will you be competing against companies from other countries importing their product into your chosen market place, but costs of these products/services/know-how will also fluctuate as the exchange rate does and you need to be in control of the situation. As we mentioned earlier, your sole motivator for exporting should be for profit.

Who to go to?

Throughout the different stages of exploration into the feasibility of exporting, you will find many organisations, both government and private, who are willing to help. As we go through the various chapters these organisations will be mentioned. For further reference their addresses will be found in Appendix IV. So whether you decide to start your research off by going to the specialised branch of your high street bank, your local chamber of commerce or the British Overseas Trade Board (BOTB), all will be willing to help and offer good, solid, hands-on advice.

Overseas markets certainly do exist, together with the facilities for reaching them. It is up to you to decide just when, where and how you can best take advantage of the

How to Export

opportunites on offer. You never know, you might be the proud winner of the next Queen's Award to Industry for achievement in the exporting field.

1
Testing The Market – Finding Out

The first step you take as a potential exporter, before spending time, effort and money on endeavouring to develop overseas sales, is to establish that there is such a demand for your product. Whether you wish to sell goods or services, it is still vital to establish that an overseas market does actually exist.

It is not generally difficult to find out the overseas market prospects for a product. If your company has a showroom or has been promoting its products at trade fairs, exhibitions and seminars in the UK, you will probably already have had some contact with overseas buyers and other foreign visitors. You should have kept yourself informed of the UK market for your product by reading the relevant sections of the trade press. Doing so will probably have given you a good idea if there is some interest in your type of product overseas.

Where to find information and advice

Once you have decided through reading, talking and listening to other people that there are export possibilities for the company's products, then is the time to assess the prospects more systematically. A good start can be made by consulting relevant books and publications in addition to making contact with people who already know the overseas market for your particular product. The central libraries in most major towns and even smaller local libraries will stock many trade and product journals and directories. The Statistics and Market Intelligence Library (the address can be found in Appendix IV) also provides detailed import and export statistics by each individual country.

In all likelihood there will be a trade association which your company can join. This will undoubtedly have an export committee which can give advice on the potential markets you are interested in. It is probable that companies with products in the same commercial or industrial sector, and who are already exporting, will give advice on export market opportunities. This is, of course, providing that your products would not be competing for the same business as theirs.

The British Overseas Trade Board (BOTB) gives excellent advice on export market opportunities. You would be well advised to make contact with your local regional office to obtain as much specific information as possible (details of addresses can be found in Appendix IV). The Export Intelligence Service (EIS) of the BOTB also publishes information regularly on a wide variety of export opportunities in many overseas markets.

Other sources of information include the international divisions of the major clearing banks and local Chambers of Commerce which have an export information service (see Appendix IV). As part of this desk research it is helpful to draw up a questionnaire detailing the information required to establish whether or not there are markets abroad which will purchase your product. This question and answer process of analysis helps to introduce a systematic approach, which is essential for success.

Carrying out market research

Once you have established that there is a market for your product, it is necessary to undertake more detailed and specific research. This will help to establish under what conditions and by what methods your product should be sold. These aspects will vary from market to market as will the sales potential in each market. Some markets may eventually not be of interest because of non-tariff barriers, unprofitable price levels, and difficulty in receiving payment for goods supplied. In general, new exporters should avoid those countries where guaranteed payment in a hard currency cannot be arranged because of foreign exchange restrictions. Many companies have experienced serious cash flow problems because of these restrictions and some have even 'gone under'.

The EEC countries are the obvious first markets for most new exporters. But do remember that VAT rates differ in member EEC countries. However, in some instances where certain types of consultancy, construction work, or goods are

Testing The Market — Finding Out

being offered, the market may be in the developing countries or in oil-producing states. Business here may be available under projects financed by aid funds with guaranteed payments. Your research at this stage should reveal whether or not there are opportunities for business under projects financed by these aid funds, for example the EEC Lome agreement and the World Bank.

There are two types of research that can be conducted at this stage: desk research and field research.

Desk research

Now that you have an idea of the market your company is looking for and the aspects of that market which need to be considered, you will probably already have in mind specific areas for consideration, and will be in a position to undertake more detailed research. As a first step you should do some general background reading about several potential markets. Appropriate supplements and articles, including economic surveys published by leading newspapers, can be found in most libraries; bank reports on export markets are available; and the *Hints to Exporters* booklets published by the BOTB can be obtained from the address found in Appendix IV.

Deciding on suitable markets

Once specific markets start to emerge as being most suitable, you will need to establish the underlying trends within them to see how they match your home market. Any differences or foreseeable problems should be highlighted.

Look for the market's growth pattern, the nature of competition both through domestic production or from overseas competition, and the distribution trends. As mentioned earlier, your main source of information will be first the BOTB, second your local chamber of commerce, and then general and business libraries. International trade and commercial directories can be located in the larger libraries. The BOTB has one of the most comprehensive collections of published information on overseas markets in the SMIL library, and a vast computerised bank of product- and industry-based information on overseas markets in their Product Data Store. With ten offices throughout the UK, the BOTB's information sources are some of the best available. Trade Associations can provide specific information for certain industries and some undertake research for that industry – for example, the furniture trade benefits in this way from the Furniture Industry Research Association.

The BOTB can also advise you about potential markets. Their market branches are in constant touch with commercial staff in UK embassies, high commissions and consulates overseas and as such have an in-depth supply of local knowledge. The BOTB can also tap the expertise of their Area Advisory Groups, each consisting of members active in business with a knowledge of trade in a particular area.

The Export Intelligence Service offered by the BOTB circulates up-to-date, computerised information on new trade opportunities throughout the world, including development projects and invitations to tender. You can subscribe to this service and opt to receive details for specific areas of the world and selected products or services. Export Network Ltd, a new on-line database system also provides this and other information for exporters.

Chambers of commerce are the other major providers of export expertise; the two largest offices being in London and Birmingham, both of which have libraries where further research can be carried out. The chambers organise and lead overseas trade missions in conjunction with the BOTB and there is generous financial assistance available to help towards meeting the cost of these trips.

The Institute of Export, formed in 1935, is not only able to give advice and assistance but also to introduce fellow exporters who have mutual interests. Again, like the chamber of commerce, the Institute has established branches in all the major centres in the UK.

Lastly, do not forget the services provided by major banks. The high street banks have set up special exporting sections whch can help in a number of ways. First, they provide assistance in marketing your product; second, they offer assistance once the sale is proceeding, ie with various types of documentation, settlements, etc.; and third, they provide economic reports which contain information on the political and economic conditions prevailing. The National Westminster Bank, for instance, published economic reports on over 70 countries. These are freely available to customers and non-customers alike. Lastly, banks can offer assistance if you are setting up a branch office overseas (although this is a route that should not be followed initially) by providing introductions and advice. Ask your local branch for the address and telephone number.

Field research

After investigating this wealth of published sources, your next step should be to undertake some original research in the field. This can be done through external market research agencies or consultants – or indeed, through your own company's personnel. The BOTB can advise on how to set about this and can also make a grant of up to 50 per cent of the cost through their Export Marketing Research Scheme. Undertaking this research yourself has the added advantage of providing you with direct experience of a market, which will be valuable at a later stage. Visiting the market on an outward mission, or attending a trade fair in conjunction with your local chamber of commerce will give you a final, all-important, first-hand experience of the market, enabling you to decide whether or not this market is the right one for you.

Selecting the right market is a significant decision, since making the wrong choice when you start could be a costly mistake. It may also lead you to the false conclusion that exporting is not for you. Whatever the outcome you must make a commercial decision which suits your business.

Trade Fairs and Exhibitions

It has to be recognised that a small business wishing to export does not have large resources of money or people to carry out detailed market research. Nevertheless, inexpensive market research can be carried out by attending international trade exhibitions and fairs in the UK and overseas. Here you can find out what your competitors are offering and how they go about selling to foreign markets. It is also a good idea to begin exporting by taking a stand at such exhibitions with the intention of securing orders. Initially, as a new exporter, you may wish to limit your attendance to international exhibitions in the UK with the aim of selling to visiting overseas buyers. This will give you some practical experience of exporting and will draw your attention to potential payment problems and the other requirements that have to be met to achieve satisfactory sales.

Methods of transport

It is not generally realised how easy it is for manufacturers and retailers to export products where the weight and size are below certain limits. The Post Office handles a very large volume of such exports to a wide variety of countries. When considering exporting you would be well advised to establish contact with your local representative of the international parcels division of the Post Office. Through them you can obtain all the necessary information on how to send parcels overseas, together with copies of the Post Office guide, the overseas compendium and SITPRO forms which will be looked at in full in Chapter 8. (These are also available at your local Post Office.)

Other services available through the Post Office include direct mailing facilities to selected groups of potential customers in certain markets. This information will enable you to determine if you can send your products to the countries you have targeted, and calculate the approximate cost of doing so. You can then sell on the basis of Cash Before Delivery (CBD) or Cash On Delivery (COD), thus ensuring you are paid for your goods. It is possible to sell to over 100 countries on a COD basis, but it may take some time before the money is transferred to you. It is also important to ensure that your goods are insured to their full value, even though they are being sent through the Post Office system.

In certain parts of the world, and especially in EEC countries and North America, there are express freight and parcel service organisations which have extensive delivery services. They will accept larger, heavier parcels than the Post Office and these organisations will handle much of the documentation and will also collect payment on a COD basis if required (see Chapter 2). This type of service is becoming increasingly important for deliveries within EEC countries, so you should obtain information about the services of such companies as part of your initial market research.

Also available are directories which provide lists of carriers who act as freight forwarders as well, and freight forwarders who only perform that single function. The latter are particularly important as they will arrange the delivery of all kinds of goods to any part of the world. The Institute of Freight Forwarders can provide a full list of approved organisations employing qualified freight forwarding staff (see also Chapter 7 and Appendix IV).

Agents

There are numerous other possibilites for the small business which wishes to begin exporting, including:

1 Trading companies in the UK which specialise in importing and exporting, many of whom are members of the Export Houses Association.

2 Buying offices, particularly in London, for companies which are engaged in the retail trade in some overseas markets.

3 Companies which have overseas manufacturing subsidiaries or associates and are looking for goods and services for these organisations.

4 A few multinational companies, such as ICI plc, which are willing to assist smaller companies. They usually do this by allowing their overseas sales offices to enter into sales agency agreements to sell products which are complementary to the ICI range.

It is only by carrying out thorough desk research, and making contact by letter and telephone with possible agents, that you will find out who might be interested in handling your products.

Pricing your product

One of the major problems you will face is how to price your product or service for the overseas market. Clearly there is a difference, sometimes a very large difference, between the total cost of a product sold on an ex-works basis and the same product sold on a delivered basis overseas. The latter has to include such additional costs as overseas freight, insurance, packaging, duties and other taxes, handling charges, agent's or other commissions and interest charges if extended payment terms are being granted. Such extra costs must be clearly established so that you can be sure that the market price, or the price at which you expect to sell, will give a reasonable profit. Determining the price of your product needs to be done as carefully in each overseas market as in the UK. There are likely to be wide variations in price between one market and another, and sometimes between different sectors of the same market.

The process of determining prices in each overseas market may be more difficult than in the UK. This may be because of language differences, lack of sales representation and perhaps the problem of funding very expensive on-the-spot market research. In developed countries it should be possible to employ a market research organisation to obtain prices and other information which will assist you in developing a marketing plan. The British Overseas Trade Board (BOTB) will provide advice and some financial assistance for market research. However, there is no doubt that a well planned visit by yourself or your representative to carefully selected potential overseas markets is likely to be the most beneficial. Such a visit may be necessary in order to find and appoint a sales agent or distributor, one of whose responsibilities must be to provide regular market information regarding the reception of your product and those of the competition.

Trade missions

One way of making an initial visit to certain markets is to join a trade mission. By doing so, the cost of such a visit is likely to be subsidised and there are bound to be experienced exporters in the party who will give you help and advice. The leader of the trade mission will have had experience in accompanying and leading other missions and his advice should be sought prior to departure.

Neighbouring European countries represent the easiest opportunities for many potential exporters. Travelling in Europe does not present serious problems and it is not difficult to employ sales agents, distributors and salesmen as you would in the UK. There are some difficulties to be overcome, for example different VAT rules and sometimes different technical requirements. In general, providing you have:

1   established that there is a market for your product,

2   ensured that there are no insurmountable difficulties in employing a suitably qualified and experienced local agent,

3 ascertained they can be supported by visits to and from your company,

you should find that sales develop successfully.

Local requirements

It is essential to ensure that the product or service you wish to promote in each of your selected markets is suited to local requirements. If you are selling fashion goods then it is vital to study the particular needs of each marketplace. Design preferences can vary considerably from country to country and even within different parts of the same country. Providing you receive sufficient feedback from the market on these specific requirements, and react sensibly and speedily to this information, you should be able to build a reputation for your goods or services.

Although most countries adopt UK standards and specifications for some of their requirements, others have their own standards which you will have to satisfy. The British Standards Institution provides a service known as Technical Help for Exporters (THE). This is run for the BOTB which offers small companies using the service for the first time a 50 per cent discount on THE's charges.

THE provides advice to enable exporters to check that their products meet the overseas technical requirements of individual markets. They provide English translations of foreign standards and specifications, relevant legislation and codes of practice. Good local agents in each overseas market will also keep you advised of any changes in technical requirements likely to affect the sales of your product or the provision of your services.

Promoting your product

The successful promotion of your product depends on having the right promotional literature, package design, advertising and instructions for each market. For example, there is no point in having everything written in English when the language of the country might be French, German, Arabic or Chinese. Not only is it important to ensure that everything is translated correctly, but you must also ensure that brand names, colours, trade marks and other designs are not in anyway offensive to potential customers. There are organisations in the UK (eg Chambers of Commerce) which specialise in translating written material into foreign languages. However, it is still sensible to have the translation finally checked by your overseas agent.

Packaging

One aspect of selling overseas which seems to cause some companies difficulties is that of packaging. Advice is available, however, from the Paper and Board, Printing and Packaging Industries Research Association (PIRA) on how to pack goods for export to protect them from damage. It will also explain what is needed to meet freight and climatic conditions, and any local regulations, eg local customs requirements. Export packaging is a highly specialised activity and there are companies which offer this service. However, it is still important to obtain reports from your local agent regarding the condition in which both your products and their packaging are being received by customers. Drums that will not stand up to the rigours of sea voyages and transport over rough roads will not endear your product to a customer, particularly if the container has spilled some of its contents by the time it arrives.

Finance

The financial terms and currency under which you may, or should sell your goods in each market have to be found out through research. Information should not only be sought in the marketplace but also from other exporters selling to that country and from the international divisions of the clearing banks. It is pointless trying to sell to customers in EEC countries on the basis of letter of credit payment in sterling, or on an ex-works basis if your competitors are selling on a delivered basis in local currency. Also, as mentioned before, it would be very foolish to sell into a country that was very short of hard currency unless you can obtain a guarantee of payment in such currency. The ability of both your customer and the country where it is located to provide payment in sterling or some other hard currency must be established.

Organisations such as Dun and Bradstreet can provide status reports on countries and credit ratings for potential customers in many of the developed countries, including those in the EEC and North America. The major clearing banks can also provide credit ratings for various countries throughout the world, including details of the average length of time it takes for payment to be made.

Insurance

You will also need to consider insurance not only for loss of your goods but also against delays in payment. The Export Credits Guarantee Department, the clearing banks and export insurance companies can assist with this requirement. In some countries, however, freight insurance has to be given to local insurance companies, which may prove to be an added problem since you will be dealing with a company which is geographically distant and does not know either you or your company.

Croner's Reference Book for Exporters gives detailed information, by country, and also supplies information of the documentary requirements regarding imported goods. This essential reference book for all exporters is produced in loose-leaf format with monthly updates and further details can be obtained from Croner Publications (see Appendix IV).

Once your export business is well developed it is worthwhile considering a computer system that can handle export documentation, and which can be linked to an information system. Information technology is advancing at a rapid rate and a number of organisations have comprehensive systems designed to meet the needs of exporters for information on markets, shipping and finance. The Institute of Export can provide this information with credit ratings by telephone and post to small companies unable to subscribe directly to on-line systems.

As a prospective exporter it is vital for you to become familiar with both published sources and organisations which can give your company advice and information. A list of these is given in Appendix IV. You will also find it essential to establish good personal contacts with individuals in other organisations who can provide advice and assistance to help you carry out your exporting in an efficient and professional manner.

2
Factors to be Considered Before Deciding to Export

Once it has been determined that there are opportunities for profitable sales in overseas markets, the next step is to take an overall view of how a decision to move into the export market will directly affect your company's existing domestic commitments and future plans. You will find that you now need to look at the practical implementation of the information your research has uncovered in order to develop a proper export strategy.

This is vitally important if you are to become an effective international trader, even if your initial intention is to develop business only in neighbouring EEC markets. Too many companies drift into exporting and then find themselves in difficulties, particularly in the areas of meeting different specifications and delivery dates and financing their overseas customers' credit.

The global market for suitable products and services is obviously much larger than the UK market. Therefore companies successful in exporting often find that their overseas trade becomes the dominant part of their business, and when this happens everyone in the company is affected. They then need to think in terms of the worldwide market, the different requirements of each separate area of that market and the effect exporting will have on the part of the business they control.

How will existing resources be affected?

As a director or owner of a small business your main concern will be the need to manage the finances of your company efficiently and profitably. If your company is 'market-led', then market strategy should be given at least the same importance as financial strategy in boardroom discussions. The impact of an export marketing strategy on every function in your business must also be considered.

Part of your responsibility must be to examine the resources which are available and necessary to support export sales and estimate their effect on cashflow and working capital. It may be necessary to make a financial investment in order to develop and establish overseas sales. For example, initial visits to overseas markets, participation in international trade fairs and exhibitions, and the preparation of literature and so on for each will require an 'up-front' financial commitment. You will control the granting of credit, decide on payment terms and the management of credit insurance. If you intend to sell on open account in local currency, on a delivered basis – for example in France – then responsibility for determining the credit status of potential customers also has to be determined.

You will have to arrange meetings with the international division of your company's bank, and agree on the handling of currency exchange problems and possible credit insurance. If cashflow is likely to be a problem in the initial stages of market development, then an increased loan may also be required. The possibility of discounting bills, factoring of debts and forfaiting should all be considered. The advantage of factoring is that the factoring company will be responsible for collecting payments from customers. It will also guarantee payment in sterling less an agreed percentage of the fee.

If you are exporting capital goods, then forfaiting should be considered. By this method the total amount owed by your customer is sold to the forfaitor for a discount. As an exporter you are paid immediately and the forfaitor collects the money owed from your buyers.

Payment by Irrevocable and Confirmed (by reputable international bank) Letters of Credit or by avalised (guaranteed by customer's bank) Bills of Exchange are other ways to make reasonably sure of receiving payment when it falls due. Both documents can be discounted for cash after acceptance by the bank if they are for payment after a credit period. It is essential that you familiarise yourself with all the financial aspects of exporting so that you can take these factors into consideration when planning marketing strategy.

All aspects of your company's business will be affected by

Factors to be Considered Before Deciding to Export

the decision to enter the export market. An evaluation of all the company's resources is essential to determine whether or not it has the capability to enter the export market. The first need is either to develop in-house expertise to handle export marketing and documentation, or to employ an export specialist to assist in both these crucial areas. If the knowledge and skills are already available amongst existing staff then you are very fortunate. It is also useful to identify any foreign language skills, both written and verbal, possessed by your staff since such skills are likely to be required as business develops.

Production

The production facilities of your company also need to be reassessed. This will ensure that not only is there sufficient spare capacity to meet export orders, but that this capacity is flexible enough to allow for changes in specifications to meet different standards. Should production be dependent on components bought in from outside suppliers, it is clearly important to check that they can meet an increased demand. One factor to remember is the need to change the language of any instructions on products being manufactured for non-English speaking markets. Those responsible for production scheduling should also be made aware of the major difficulties that can arise if shipments are not made by the date stipulated on letters of credit.

Packing and labelling

Those responsible for packing the goods will also have to acquire new knowledge and skills about packing and labelling for export markets. However, specialist export packing companies can be employed for specific shipments, or training arranged for staff if no expertise already exists in your company.

Documentation

If freight forwarders are being used to arrange the transport of goods, then advice can be obtained from them on packing and labelling as well as documentation requirements. Although specialists can be employed on a part-time basis to do all the documentation, it is essential that a full-time member of staff is trained to understand export documentation. There are many one- or two-day courses available to help employees acquire an understanding of this documentation. The Institute of Export and your Chamber of Commerce will run such courses as do Dun and Bradstreet and a number of other training companies.

However, if you decide that your company will handle all its own documentation then, depending on the timescale you are working to, you will either have to recruit someone with previous exporting knowledge or arrange for a member of your existing staff to undertake in-depth training. In order to acquire the appropriate knowledge and understanding they can either study for the Institute of Export's Certificate in Export Office Practice or undertake the Institute's Foundation Course in Overseas Trade. Full details of these and their other export courses can be obtained from the Institute at the address shown in Appendix IV.

What additional resources will be needed?

When this audit has been completed you may find that your company already has sufficient resources to develop its exporting strategy. But if this is not the case then it is likely that substantial additional finance will be required to provide them. If such finance is not readily available you should consider putting your business development plan to selected venture capital companies. A number of such organisations are now actively looking for investment opportunities with companies wishing to develop their exporting capability.

Payment terms

The old adage that a sale has not been completed until you have received full payment is particularly apt for the export business. Many small companies have learnt through bitter experience the importance of taking every reasonable precaution to ensure that the customer pays in accordance with agreed terms.

The financial and competitive situation in each market will usually dictate the terms of payment that should be offered at any given time. For example, should a particular market economy deteriorate and become short of hard currency, it would be prudent to adopt terms that guarantee payment in a hard currency, even if your competitors have not yet hardened

Factors to be Considered Before Deciding to Export

their terms. It is also unwise to offer longer credit periods for payment than your competitors in order to obtain sales. They will quickly negate any such advantage by simply matching your terms. In general, particularly for a small firm, it is better to concentrate on giving better quality and service to beat the competition, rather than trying to secure a short-term advantage by offering easier methods of payment or longer periods of credit.

In some instances, however, your buyer may want to pay in a currency other than sterling. Provided such payment is made in another hard currency (for example, Deutsch Marks, French francs, CFA francs, US dollars and other currencies of EEC countries) you should accept assuming, of course, that it is still a profitable business. Your banks will offer assistance in handling payment in foreign currencies. They can also protect you against exchange-rate fluctuations by the forward selling of the expected total payment, thus enabling you to know the actual net amount of sterling you will earn on each transaction.

If you expect to do business in Western European countries in local currencies you should investigate the system in use by the Giro banks. In some countries this currently appears to have advantages over the normal clearing bank system. For example, the Giro bank system claims that money is transferred to the exporter's account more quickly than through the clearing bank systems, and that the charges for most aspects of the payment transaction are fixed. Thus, you would be able to include reasonably accurate costs in your price calculations. It is always tempting for a new exporter to insist on guaranteed payment terms, regardless of the conditions in the market and the credit status of the buyer. Clearly, selling on the basis of CBD (Cash Before Delivery) or COD (Cash on Delivery) via the Post Office or express freight services is one way of securing payment. Selling on the basis of avalised Bills of Exchange (guaranteed by the customer's bank) or against Irrevocable and Confirmed Letters of Credit, with collection of payment through your own bank or another acceptable bank, is also reliable provided all documentation is strictly correct.

It is not always possible to sell on guaranteed payment terms, particularly to customers in Western Europe and North America. So you can either sell through a reliable stockist or distributor who purchases your goods for resale, or sell direct to the customer for payment after delivery, in local currency through an open account. The situation with regard to payment risks is then, in fact, very little different from the UK market. It is therefore essential to obtain a credit status report for each potential buyer from a reputable credit rating agency and a banker's reference from your customer's bank.

Even if you are satisfied with the status of a potential customer and therefore willing to sell on open account, it may still be necessary to give some credit. Payment of 30 days or of one month from the date of invoice is not uncommon and you may wish to protect yourself further against any inability to pay. The most common method of insuring against such failure is to take out an insurance policy either directly with ECGD (Export Credits Guarantee Department), via a clearing bank, or with an export credit insurance company. It is important to investigate all available methods of credit insurance during the course of your initial market research.

Transport

The various methods of transporting your goods to customers, their costs and delivery terms all need to be evaluated in order to determine the least expensive and most reliable method. It may be more important to get the goods to the customer in a sound condition than, for example to deliver in 48 hours. Discussion in advance with a good freight forwarder who is a member of the Institute of Freight Forwarders or one of the other freight forwarding institutes will provide much of the information required to enable you to determine your needs. You should discuss cargo insurance with the freight forwarder since insuring your goods against loss or damage is essential (see Chapter 6). It is important to ensure that the goods are recovered up to the point where your customer has legally become owner and takes over responsibility for both their insurance and payment. The freight forwarder will produce most of the export documents for you if you are unable to do this yourself.

Internal administration

The internal planning and management of production, packing and despatch of goods for export, together with the appropriate documentation, has to be carefully controlled to avoid delivery delays, payment failures and other costly mistakes. You must ensure that effective methods of

Factors to be Considered Before Deciding to Export

progressing orders through your company are used, otherwise innumerable additional problems will arise. For example, Letters of Credit normally call for shipment by a certain date. If delivery for shipment is delayed beyond that point and the Bills of Lading date runs out, it will not be possible to obtain payment against the Letter of Credit unless the latest shipment date on this document is amended by the buyers (an amendment which is not always easy to obtain).

Efficient administration is vital to the success of any export policy. You will either need to employ experienced staff who understand all aspects of export documents, or arrange training for an existing member of staff. Short one- to three-day courses in export documentation are provided by most local Chambers of Commerce and, as previously mentioned, the Institute of Export runs more detailed courses.

Sales and marketing

The export marketing and selling operations in any small business usually have to be carried out by a limited number of people. They must not only control the activities of any salesmen, sales agents or distributors overseas, but also process and manage all the usual transactions dealt with in a sales office. Every order must be vetted, checked and progressed until final payment has been received.

In the absence of an export marketing manager you will have a key role to play in ensuring your company does not take on sales commitments beyond its resources. Equally you will need to assist all other departments in recognising the impact export sales business will have on their resource requirements. Forecasting, budgeting and monitoring are also an essential part of the job. Any other managers in your organisation will also be dependent on you for information to enable them to do their forecasting and planning, particularly those concerned with production.

The appointment of sales agents, distributors, stockists and salesmen in overseas markets will also fall to you. It is essential that you are aware of the standard forms of contract to be used in the appointment of overseas agents and personnel. Although the Institute of Export can provide information on contract terms it is essential to obtain the advice of experts in this area, some multinational companies may be willing to assist, as will some international firms of solicitors. However, good local advice is always worth obtaining.

You will also need to become aware of any special aspects in relation to payment terms, for example special rebates or discounts. If you appoint a good agent he should advise you of any special problems or payment arrangements peculiar to that market. The agent should also advise on any variation in selling conditions needed to satisfy that country's legal requirements. Selling conditions should always be printed on the back of proforma invoices or tender offers, so that there can be no doubt the buyer is aware of them. These conditions should always include an arbitration clause to allow for settlement of disputes. Such a clause should stipulate either the London Court of International Arbitration or the ICC, International Court of Arbitration in Paris.

Keeping in touch

Effective communications with those representing your company overseas as well as with overseas buyers is vital. For most countries – but not all – the telephone, telex and postal systems are perfectly adequate methods for regular communication. They should be supplemented by periodic visits to the country concerned to meet agents, and existing and potential customers. In general it is only by making such visits that a proper understanding and feel for a market can be acquired. In fact, this is part of every exporter's market research role, as it enables you not only to keep up to date with the requirements of your customers and agents but also to study the activities of your competitors. This market research must include a study of all the aspects of a product – its packaging, methods of storage and delivery, publicity literature, instructive literature and commercial terms. You will also be able to carry out an on-the-spot assessment of the performance of your selling agents.

Your trip should include visits to any banks which will be concerned with payment transactions. It is also a good idea to call on the commercial section of the British Embassy or Consulate and other organisations which are able to assist you (eg the British Chamber of Commerce office).

The promotion of export sales on a continuous basis needs to be carefully planned, successes and failures monitored, and the performance of sales agents regularly assessed. Customers' accounts need to be managed just as they would in the UK to ensure that orders are being delivered on time, payment is

Factors to be Considered Before Deciding to Export

being received and replacement orders being made at anticipated intervals. If a customer is buying on an open account it is important to have a debt-chasing system which may, after an appropriate interval, include the use of a debt-collecting agency or claims against your credit insurance. Effective systems of control must be developed and maintained.

In a small business you are likely to be responsible for both UK and export sales with administrative assistance on export documentation. It is vital that all those who are to be responsible for export administration have a proper understanding of the nature and importance of the documentation involved. Correct handling of the documentation required when exporting is just as important as the marketing and financial aspects. The chief executive in any business has a responsibility to his company, its employees and customers to ensure that all these functions are properly performed to the benefit of the business.

Lastly, it is also vital for the person who is going abroad to sell your company's product to have sufficient authority vested in him to make decisions whilst he is there. Sadly, in the UK, we lose out to foreign competitors because decision-making has to be referred back to the head office in the UK. Even if this information is sent by telex or cable delays do take place, allowing competitors to take a firm and decisive order. If you do not have sufficient trust in your sales person or team, then it is pointless sending them out to sell your company's products.

Before sending out a representative, make sure that he is thoroughly briefed and all possible questions have been answered. Make contingency plans by setting up a rapid system of referral should any unforeseen question arise.

3
To Which Countries Should I Export?

There is no shortage of choices when selecting an overseas market – listing the overseas countries to which the UK exports goods and services produces a lengthy gazeteer of the world. Of these countries there are 180 where UK exports exceed the value of £1 million each year, a clear indication of the potential for UK exporters. But the choice can be bewildering. Other than by sticking a pin in a map of the world, how does the company new to exporting choose which countries it should export to?

Once you have established that your company is in a position to export, your first step will be to take stock of your present situation. The nature of your home market, your company's resources, the nature of your product and how it is used, the market size and level of development and the environment required for its operation and any knowledge of the envisaged market. Using this knowledge you can build up a profile of your potential overseas market. By listing the characteristics of your UK market in terms of buying habits, incomes, lifestyles and any other factors affecting it, you can look for similar characteristics in overseas markets and hope to build on your home market success. Ultimately your market is not a particular country but the potential purchasers of your product or service wherever they live. You should therefore have a clear idea of who these people are before deciding on which geographical area to concentrate.

If you can find these customers in a market which operates under similar conditions to those in the UK, you will be starting your exporting effort on a sound basis. No two markets are quite the same, but the more familiar you are with a potential overseas market the better you are placed to interpret the prevailing trends for trade and the successful promotion of your product. It may seem simplistic but, on the same basis, looking at countries you know from visits or holidays abroad can be a good starting point. An understanding of a way of life in a certain country will greatly assist you in your task of deciding how to sell your goods there.

Market research will uncover the real potential for your product and your chances of success in a particular market, and is therefore a vital part of the process of starting to export.

However, it is clearly neither feasible nor sensible to research every market. Combining your knowledge of the conditions needed for your business to thrive with a background knowledge of conditions in markets around the world will help narrow the field considerably. Market conditions are affected by geographic, cultural and economic factors, all of which should be taken into account before making your selection.

Access

You will need to consider whether a market is geographically accessible. The nearer a market is to the UK the easier it will be to visit and to service. This is no small consideration for a business exporting for the first time. You may not have the resources at hand to service a market at the other side of the world, neither in financial terms or time spent travelling. Furthermore, when problems do emerge they may seem daunting if they are at a great distance from the UK. In addition, spreading your market too wide geographically can bring problems of servicing, which is a good reason for concentrating your efforts on one or two countries, rather than spreading your resources too thinly. Your geographical knowledge will enable you to take distance into account when planning export strategy. For example, it is wiser to start exporting to one state in the USA and build up your business from there, rather than trying to tackle the whole USA market. Remember the distance from New York to San Francisco is the same as that from London to New York!

Then there are the conditions of terrain and climate which may present other difficulties, or have implications for the sales or distribution of your particular product. If the terrain makes distribution of goods difficult this factor must be weighed against the advantages of that particular market for

To Which Countries Should I Export?

your product. Should your goods be affected by extremes of temperature your choice of market will be limited accordingly.

Language and culture

Another area you must also consider, particularly if you are looking at the Middle and Far East, is that of cultural differences. Whichever country you decide to export to the most obvious obstacle will be that of language. Your own facility or that of your staff in the languages of your chosen markets may be a crucial factor. If you feel that you can just 'get by' in any particular market using English, you should remember that at some stage you will need to produce sales literature and packaging in the local language. Ideally you should be familiar with the language of your export market, or it should be one where English is an acceptable, commonly used business language. Therefore if you are unfamiliar with export procedures you will be safer opting for a country which has codes of business practice similar to those of the UK, since cultural differences can make business transactions confusing.

There are also a whole range of social, practical and religious differences which need to be considered. These factors will not affect all exporters to the same degree and many may only come to light as a result of more detailed market research. At the early stage of selecting a market you will, for example, dismiss the idea of selling alcohol to the Middle East. However, too many assumptions cannot be made as proved by the UK company which succeeded in selling sand to Saudi Arabia!

Tariffs and trade blocs

Whether or not a market is economically accessible is obviously important. Tariff and non-tariff barriers operate throughout the world to a greater or lesser extent. You will need to know in the early stages of selecting a market what tariffs apply. For instance, customs duties on goods are imposed by most countries which, depending on their severity, can make your goods less competitive than those produced locally. For example, Japan's highly restrictive import practices have caused considerable ill will throughout the years, particularly in the USA, but also in other countries.

How to Export

Non-tariff barriers might, for example, include restrictions on the amount of foreign currency an importer has available to pay for goods. In some cases it may be necessary to obtain an import licence which, once again, can be used to restrict the nature of goods imported. In addition, some countries impose specific regulations on imported goods, as in the case of china products entering the USA which must have no lead content.

Trading blocs around the world bring standardised trading practices to groups of countries. As a member of the EEC the UK is able to sell goods within the Community without having to pay customs duty. This also applies to countries with whom the EEC has special arrangements, such as Austria and Sweden. The Council for Mutual Economic Assistance (COMECON) is the trading bloc which covers the communist countries, including Eastern Europe and Cuba. Here all trade decisions are made by the State, with whose representatives the exporter must meet. Research into the needs or requirements of those countries within COMECON is not allowed.

You will not be surprised to learn, given these considerations, that most of the UK's exports are directed to the markets of Western Europe and North America, with the greater share going to the USA, Canada, Germany, France and the Netherlands. Western Europe receives 60 per cent of our goods and is an excellent choice for the first-time exporter. These countries are easily reached from the UK and are of similar structure, with highly affluent, developed markets displaying similar trends of consumer spending and accounting for around half of the world's total imports. Some of them will already be familiar to you as you may have visited them on holiday and have some understanding of their way of life – you may even have some contacts there. In addition, the marketplace is basically tariff-free. All these factors will give added confidence to the new exporter.

European markets are extremely accessible to UK exporters but the markets of North America and Australia may be attractive in other ways. They speak the same language and have similar cultures, facts which help to balance the disadvantages of tariffs and the long distances involved. No one can tell you to which country you should export because there is no single ideal market. Your choice of market will depend on your company's resources and the sales opportunities which exist.

To Which Countries Should I Export?

You can establish which are the largest and most accessible markets but they may not necessarily be the best ones for your company. Statistics which show a country that has a high level of imports also indicate a willingness to accept exports. However, in such a situation there may be many companies competing for the same business. Your ideal market is the one that offers the best opportunities with the minimum of competition. However, just because there are complications involved in exporting to a particular market is no reason to discount it, if your research shows that it offers good opportunities for your product. You do need to be fully aware of the implications of exporting there and know enough about the problems involved to be sure that you have the resources to deal with them. For example, there are bound to be greater opportunities for some products in the countries of the Middle East and Africa than in Western Europe. However, it is well known that some of these countries have slow and tedious border control procedures or may present payment problems, as do other developing countries such as India and Latin America.

Payment

Although payment difficulties cannot always be anticipated you should establish, as far as is possible, the likelihood of this occurring and be aware of those countries with foreign currency restrictions. To some extent risks can be alleviated by taking out credit insurance through ECGD or private sector companies. For smaller businesses, the banks and other export finance companies offer ECGD-backed cover through their schemes. As a general rule, exporting to a high-risk country should be avoided by the new exporter. In some cases, as in Brazil, exporting certain products is out of the question due to the restrictions imposed. The only alternative open to the exporter is to set up a local manufacturing base through a joint venture with a local domestic company.

One of the major areas to watch out for when invoicing for products/services supplied is that of invoicing in foreign currencies. Foreign exchanges have in the past been noted as 'the wilder beasts in the export jungle', and for the first-time exporter in particular this is an area which should be avoided. Try if possible to invoice in pounds sterling. However, this can and often does lead to the displeasure from your overseas

How to Export

buyer. If you do decide to risk the currency market and invoice in the currency of the country to which you are exporting (the degree of risk is termed 'foreign exchange exposure'), then this means that while you know the rate of exchange on the day the contracts are signed you will not know the rate applying at the time the contracts are exchanged. In order to minimise the risk you have three options: a foreign currency account, a forward exchange contract or a foreign currency borrowing facility.

Foreign currency accounts mean that you will have to open a bank account in that foreign currency through which income and expenditure can go. Basically, it eliminates the risk by matching your currency receivable against your expenditure. However, this is very tricky and rarely will you be able to do it. Another method of risk-reduction should be considered to operate in tandem with this system.

A forward exchange contract is the more usual method and is available through all the clearing banks. It operates as follows. You arrange a contract to sell the currency you receive to the bank at a future stipulated date (a fixed contract) or more usually between two fixed dates (option contract). The option extends only to delivery of the currency, and there are penalties if the contract has not been used by the time it matures. Early contact with your bank is essential if you wish to crystallise your exchange risk by using this method.

However, before entering into any currency commitments do ensure that a market exists for the currency, the amount specified and the time period stated.

Foreign currency borrowing

The third method is not as well known but should also be considered. It should only apply if you are invoicing in a strong currency – which the pound sterling is at the time of going to press. However, sterling does tend to fluctuate, a fact which should be checked at the time this method is under consideration.

If you are able to quantify your currency needs over a period of, say, six months then you can borrow that amount from your bank and exchange it for sterling on the same day at the rate of exchange ruling on that day (known as the 'spot' rate). The sterling equivalent can then be used to reduce your sterling overdraft or be applied as working capital. Once you

To Which Countries Should I Export?

have received payment in the foreign currency you can then apply the amount to reducing your currency borrowing. However, you must have foreign currency income from your export receivables to repay the borrowing, otherwise you will achieve what you set out to avoid – a loss through foreign exchange exposure.

As a rule of thumb to decide whether or not a currency is strong, low interests rates are usually associated with strong currencies, ie the Swiss franc.

The City of London is one of the major exchanges in the world where spot and forward currencies can be bought and sold. (Some 26 currencies are traded every day in London.)

When starting off in exporting, should you have a number of outlets in the world market, then select two or at most three currencies, which are generally accepted throughout the world, and stick to those using the above methods if necessary to reduce your exchange risk.

A point to remember here is, should you be selling to Hong Kong, and using the US dollar as the transaction currency then you need to bear in mind not only the fluctuation between the Hong Kong dollar and the US dollar but also between the US dollar and the pound sterling.

How to avoid bad debts

If you follow the general principles which you use in the UK but add a few as noted below then you should be able to avoid bad debts.

Do not get too excited if you receive an unsolicited order from overseas, and most certainly do not just despatch the goods. Increasingly, these orders are arriving accompanied by fraudulent guaranteed payment orders or letters; and many are sophisticated. Courteously write or telex back stating that you normally require letters of reference, but as the time does not allow for this then you require an irrevocable letter of credit payable against a London bank. This method is the safest and should be used as the standard one.

In risky markets it is always better to ask for a letter of credit. Talk to the Export Credits Guarantee Department and provided that you take the normal precautions you can then insure for 90 to 95 per cent of the risk.

When checking out references sent in by overseas companies, ask the BOTB or the exporting section of your high street bank for help in confirming their validity.

How to Export

Always be careful to check the status of the country you export to. The companies ordering your goods may be bona fide, but the country in which they are located may have a large foreign debt and implement restricted foreign currency payment. In some African and Central/South American countries payments can take as long as 27 to 30 months – there have been instances of even longer periods!

4
Opening Up Export Markets

Once you have selected your overseas market, how do you go about developing it? What steps should you take to obtain sales? Of course, it is possible to try and sell direct to potential customers either by using mail-shots or by advertising in appropriate journals. These methods are not normally effective, however, unless combined with other marketing activities, such as visiting the market yourself or appointing local agents or distributors. Potential customers are not likely to be willing to order a product from a manufacturer they have never heard of, situated hundreds or possibly thousands of miles away, if there is no local representatives to sort out any problems that may arise. Direct mail campaigns to overseas markets need to be coordinated with on-the-spot action.

What Kind of Sales Organisation?

Some kind of sales network must also be set up, and the following options are those which you will need to consider:

1   Regularly visiting the market yourself.
2   Sending out a member of your sales staff.
3   Using export merchants or export managers in the UK.
4   Appointing local agents or distributors.
5   Setting up a branch sales office abroad.
6   Licensing a local firm to produce goods to your company's design.
7   Establishing a subsidiary or associate company abroad with its own manufacturing and marketing divisions.

Let us now look at these possibilities in more detail, to ensure that you make the right decision for your company:

How to Export

1 It is certainly advisable to visit the overseas market, but not really practical to rely on this as a sole selling method. For the more complex type of transaction, the customer may expect to see you as you will be able to make immediate decisions about prices and delivery dates.

2 This is only a realistic possibility if you can afford to have this salesperson in the overseas market for several months each year. Such a salesperson should report back on a weekly basis, but must also have sufficient knowledge and authority to answer questions and make on-the-spot decisions.

3 Export merchants/confirming houses/commission agents in the UK operate in various ways, often under the same roof. They buy goods outright and sell on their own behalf, confirm orders received from abroad (ie take care of the financial arrangements) and arrange shipment and insurance for the overseas buyer. Most specialise in particular overseas markets and/or goods. A development of this approach is the export management company. They act as the manufacturer's own export department, taking care of every aspect of the procedure from trying to locate potential customers, through arranging suitable payment terms, to shipping and documentation. These firms will handle the products of a number of small manufacturers. There are also buying offices in London which specialise in purchasing goods suitable for departments and chain stores located in the USA and a number of other countries.

There are obvious advantages in using a UK-based export agent or merchant. You are dealing with a business located in the same country as yourself. It can handle packing if necessary, arrange shipment and would normally prepare any special export documents which might be required. However, you must also consider the main disadvantage that you, the manufacturer, are not in direct touch with the customer and therefore have much less control. In the long-term this may prove totally unacceptable, although it can work for makers of standard items such as hardware, fasteners, tools and consumer goods.

4 Appointing a local agent or distributor is the most common method of opening up an export market. There are two principal types:

(a) the commission agent who will book orders on your behalf, with you issuing invoices direct to the customer and

(b) the importer/distributor, who will buy from you on his own account and then fix his own price levels.

Which type you choose depends on a number of factors, including the type of product you are selling, the custom of the market you are selling into and your experience in the home market.

Finding a suitable agent is not easy, as you may already know from trying to locate sales outlets in the UK. There are several ways and it is suggested that you investigate them all. You can use the BOTB's Export Representative Service. This service employs the experience and knowledge of Commercial Councillors at the British High Commissions, Embassies or Consulates in the country concerned. Your initial approach should be made through your local regional office of the BOTB (see Appendix IV).

Your local Chamber of Commerce will also be able to help, through the network of British Chambers of Commerce abroad as well as other local chambers. Most of these send regular newsletters to their members in which brief details of your company and its products can be published.

There are associations of manufacturers' agents and importers in some countries and particularly in the EEC. They will also advertise enquiries from overseas firms. Your bank should be able to assist through its overseas contacts.

Once you have located a suitable agent you must check him out, preferably by making a personal visit. Before signing any agreement you must examine current agency legislation for the country concerned, as it is often much easier to appoint an agent than to dismiss him. If he is located in an EEC country, consideration must be given to Article 85 of the Treaty of Rome, regarding exclusivity. It is advisable to have a written agency agreement and this should contain at least the following basic points:

— Names and addresses of principal and agent.
— Description of the goods.
— Area covered by the agreement.
— Responsibilities of the principal.
— Responsibilities of the agent.
— Rate of commission to be paid.
— If stockist-type agent, how and when goods are to be paid.

– Responsibility for advertising, sales leaflets, and other promotional matters.
– Termination of agreement, and any compensation payable.
– Law governing the agreement and arbitration, should a dispute arise.

Obviously this is not a complete list of subjects which should be considered for incorporation into an agency agreement, and much will depend on the nature of your product and the customs and practice of the trade concerned. Any agreement should always be drawn up by your company's solicitors.

Agents need to be kept in the picture and so you must offer effective back-up, for example technical support and literature. Regular visits are essential to sort out any problems, explain new products and take the opportunity to meet major customers together with your agent.

5 If the export market develops satisfactorily, you may eventually want to set up your own overseas sales office. It is easier to keep this under the direct control of head office and British personnel. Your company would need to check on the tax liabilities of such a branch, and the exchange control rules governing repatriation of profits. Also, you will need to ascertain the employment regulations for both local employees and British nationals. Work permits may be required for the latter and it is as well to ensure that these will be available to your company's personnel.

6 Alternatively, you may wish to consider the feasability of granting a local firm (possibly the original agent) a licence to manufacture your products in that country, purchasing a company already involved in similar activities or setting up your own manufacturing operation. Your final decision may well depend on the various incentives available from central or local government to encourage new manufacturing concerns in that area.

Import restrictions and duties, limits on royalty fees and withholding taxes on profits will all have to be taken into consideration when venturing into this kind of operation. However, these complications probably lie a little too far into the future for the average small company moving into the export field.

Arranging Field Visits

Once a decision has been made about the most suitable type of overseas sales network, you will then have to consider how to support your agent, distributor or branch office, principally by making personal visits to them. Such a visit can be made either on your own or with a trade mission organised by a body such as a Chamber of Commerce or Trade Association, which may be sponsored by the BOTB.

Visits are necessary because personal contact with agents and customers is most important. Even if you do not speak the language fluently, one or two words will go a long way to ease negotiations. Preparation is essential, including desk research on the market. Notification to your local BOTB office is recommended so that they can advise their overseas posts, who in turn will prepare lists of contacts for you. Your local Chamber of Commerce can help in the same way, by writing in advance to their counterparts in the overseas markets.

Check on public holidays, local industrial holidays, social customs, travel and health requirements and similar mundane but important points. You will find the *Hints to Exporters* booklets very useful as sources for such information. They are provided free of charge to exporters by the BOTB.

Once these preparations have been made advise your agent and existing and potential customers of your intended visit. It is also a good idea to send them leaflets in their own language, but the actual translation must be undertaken by someone whose language is the mother tongue, in order to achieve the desired effect.

Whilst these comments will generally apply to all kinds of business trips, sales missions organised by your local Chamber of Commerce will mean a slightly different approach. If you contemplate joining such a mission, much of the preliminary spade-work will be done by the organisers and the British posts abroad. For a beginner, therefore, this can be a very much easier way of entering the export market. For example, in 1986 Birmingham Chamber of Commerce and Industry sent out 13 missions to 18 countries and brought back orders worth £71 million.

There are several obvious advantages to being part of such an outward sales mission. Contacts are arranged for you with potential customers or agents; the mission and its members are given publicity overseas in newspapers, magazines, TV, and so on; you are with people who know the market and can give advice if problems occur and finally, but not least important, you may be eligible for a grant towards the cost.

The availability of such grants depends on the country involved. At the present time BOTB subvention is not available for missions to USA and Canada, South Africa and Western Europe (excluding Spain, Portugal, Iceland and Finland). For those areas where financial assistance is not provided there may still be Chamber-organised trips, where the other advantages still hold good.

Channels of Communication

As we have seen, communication with agents or customers is all important. If they do not hear from you regularly they will feel isolated and more inclined to promote their other lines. But apart from the postal services, what other methods of communication are open to you? In this electronic age, it may be easier to make contact by telex and facsimile transmission. Many firms overseas actually prefer these methods since they provide instantaneous hard copies of the information being transmitted and avoid potential postal delays. For those companies who do not have their own telex and fax facilities, agencies exist which offer these services on a subscription basis. They can be found in your local *Yellow Pages* under Telex Bureaux or Office Services. Fax is rapidly catching up with telex in popularity. It is now being used to send letters and other written documents and not, as in the past, just drawings and specifications which could not be transmitted on a telex machine. The cost involved in using either method is roughly comparable.

Should you need to telephone your agent, do remember to check the time difference, bearing in mind British Summertime and any similar daylight-saving scheme in the overseas country involved. Do not forget potential language problems. Arrange for a linguist to be on hand if the person whom you are telephoning is not fluent in English.

You will undoubtedly also need to use postal communications and purchasing a copy of the *Post Office Guide* will prove a good investment. This is a comprehensive directory of all the available postal services, including notes on sending letters and parcels abroad, cash-on-delivery, insurance, and so on. If you need to send literature or small samples through the post this guide is essential reading.

Advice and Assistance

Let us now discuss briefly those organisations which can help the potential exporter. Some of these we have already mentioned in connection with sales missions and location of agents, but it is as well to summarise the parts they play in assisting companies to open up overseas markets.

BOTB

The British Overseas Trade Board has a range of services, which are discussed in more detail in Chapter 1. Some of these services are free but others have to be paid for. When arranging overseas visits their help is invaluable, since they have a large number of commercial staff overseas who can supplement the information available to you in the UK. Their booklet *Help for Exporters* which can be obtained free of charge from regional offices of the BOTB, gives full details.

Chambers of Commerce

Chambers of Commerce also offer a wide range of services to the exporter. The larger Chambers have reference libraries where the names and addresses of overseas contacts can be found. Through their network abroad the Chamber can obtain additional information very quickly. Letters of introduction can be provided, as well as the ATA Carnets which you will need if taking samples with you. These documents avoid the necessity of paying import duties and taxes when entering the overseas country. They are accepted in many overseas countries (but not all) and no additional documentation is required. For EEC countries an alternative form of Carnet is now available. The EEC Customs Carnet, obtainable from HM Customs and Excise Offices is, however, somewhat restricted as to use and type of goods covered.

Banks

Your bank can also help in a number of ways, particularly with financing the overseas sale. It can supply the names of overseas contacts and provide financial reports on potential agents, if details of their bankers are known. Most banks issue economic reports on the major markets which will help you with your initial research. They can also help with travel arrangements by providing travellers cheques, foreign currency, passport applications, visas and travel insurance.

Travel Agents

A good commercial travel agent will normally provide a comprehensive business service. He will book hotels and make all the necessary travel arrangements both to and from your destination, and within the overseas territory as required. You can also obtain advice from them on health requirements, visas, travel and medical insurance cover.

Motoring Organisations

If you intend to drive yourself, do seek the advice of one of the motoring organisations with regard to local regulations and laws. For example, do you need a Green Card, or an International Driving Licence? Also make sure that you have adequate insurance to cover the vehicle and any samples you have with you as unfortunately thefts of cars and their contents also occur abroad.

Other Agencies

Foreign Embassies and Overseas Chambers with offices in London may also be able to help plan your visit. In practice, however, the level of assistance tends to vary. You may find yourself being referred back to the BOTB when they realise you wish to sell to their country not buy from it!

Other bodies which may be able to help you plan your trip include trade associations and export clubs. The Technical Help to Exporters' Section of the British Standards Institution can advise you on any technical requirements in the country concerned. It is as well to check, although these will probably already be known to you through your local contacts and existing business in the UK. It is generally true that you should build your export business on the basis of a sound home market.

In conclusion, what should be your aim in trying to export? Why attempt something which is obviously fraught with all kinds of difficulties? Hopefully you will be able to increase production, reduce unit costs, become more competitive and spread the risks by dealing with more than one market, so

Opening Up Export Markets

making your company more profitable. These should be your ultimate aims but they are unlikely to be achieved in the short term. Successful exporting is a long-term commitment, and initially it will take time, money and hard work to get established. However, do not be deterred. Remember, there is still a worldwide demand for British goods and all those organisations mentioned in this chapter exist to offer you every assistance and support.

5
Getting Paid

Getting paid promptly for the goods or services you provide to a customer in the UK has its own problems. Before supplying your goods to a UK customer you will have considered their standing, how much credit should be allowed, their reputation and track record for paying on time. Should problems arise the telephone is to hand and, if need be, you can jump into your car and meet the customer face to face to resolve the problem.

The logistics of dealing with someone on the other side of the Channel, or perhaps even the other side of the world, present much greater problems. Not only distance needs to be taken into account but also the fact that you may have to communicate in a foreign language, handling foreign currencies, while possibly coping with different standards and measurements. Furthermore, in some instances the countries involved may not be as economically or politically stable as your home market.

It is important at the outset, therefore, for you to negotiate the most secure method of payment you can, bearing in mind, of course, the need to remain competitive. Any exporter would prefer to be paid before sending the goods, whilst the importer would prefer not to pay until after he has sold them. An acceptable arrangement regarding the method of payment somewhere between the two will have to be agreed. Therefore, it is most important to be aware of the methods of payment you might encounter when selling abroad. In this way you can relate the risk involved to the standing of your buyer and the country he operates in. Basically there are four methods of payment which are listed below in order of preference:

1 Payment in Advance.
2 Payment by Irrevocable Documentary Letter of Credit.
3 Payment by Documentary Collection (sometimes called Bills of Exchange).
4 Payment on Open Account.

There is also a fifth way which is by barter or countertrade. Where export sales are made conditional upon an undertaking to accept manufactured goods, raw materials or commodities from the overseas market in settlement. Although countertrade is gaining in importance, it is unlikely that the smaller exporter would become involved, particularly at the outset.

Selection of the most appropriate method from the basic four mentioned above will depend on a variety of factors. These include the standing of the respective buyer, competitive pressures, country risk and the degree of security required by both parties. Let us now look at each method in more detail, to assist you in making the right selection for your company.

Payment in Advance

This is obviously the most attractive way to be paid, but it means that, in effect, the buyer is extending credit to the exporter. It therefore follows that this is a somewhat unusual practice, unless the exporter is selling a unique product into a market where there is limited competition. In the case of large contracts where goods have to be specially made, it is sometimes possible to negotiate a percentage payment in advance. In these circumstances the buyer very often requires an 'Advance Payment Guarantee', to be given by the exporter's bank. The bank will require security for the guarantee and will charge a fee for the service. If the contract is not completed, then the guarantee will be called and the bank will look to the exporter for its money.

If your advance payment takes the form of a cheque payable abroad, do remember that your bank will have to clear the cheque before they credit your account and this may take 21 days or more. Payment in advance is fine if you ensure you have clean money on your account unencumbered by an Advance Payment Guarantee.

Getting Paid

The Documentary Letter of Credit

This is usually the most secure and prompt method of payment but it can involve the most headaches.

A Documentary Credit can be defined in simple terms as a written undertaking given by a bank on behalf of a buyer to pay the seller an amount of money within a specific time, provided the seller presents documents to the bank, strictly in accordance with the terms and conditions laid down in the Letter of Credit. In other words, the buyer effectively provides the seller with a guarantee of payment, in return for an assurance from a bank that the required documentation has been delivered to that bank's satisfaction. It is important to note that banks deal only in documents and not in goods. They cannot be concerned with the underlying sales contract, but determine whether the terms and conditions of a credit have been met on the basis of documents alone.

There are three types of Documentary Credit – the Revocable Credit, the Irrevocable Credit, and the Irrevocable Confirmed Credit.

1 Revocable Credits are, as the name implies, credits which can be cancelled or amended by an importer (or an exporter) up to the point where the goods are shipped and documents presented to the paying bank. As such, they should be avoided and in fact are rarely used.

2 An Irrevocable Credit means that the obligations of both parties to the credit cannot be altered in any way, without the agreement of both the buyer and the seller.

When contract terms are negotiated for settlement by Létter of Credit, the buyer requests his bank (the opening bank) to open a credit in favour of the buyer (the beneficiary). If his bank is prepared to extend a facility for this purpose, then it will instruct a bank in the exporter's country to advise the exporter that the credit has been established and will incorporate details of the terms and conditions which must be fulfilled in order to obtain payment. What this means is that the opening bank stands between the buyer and seller, guaranteeing payment subject to the necessary conditions being fulfilled.

This is perfectly acceptable and quite normal when dealing with a reputable bank in a politically and economically sound country. However, you may not have heard of the bank and the country involved may well have debt problems, or there may be concern over its political stability. What you would really like is someone you can trust standing between you and the overseas bank taking on responsibility for guaranteeing the credit. In these circumstances you could ask for the credit to be confirmed by a UK clearing bank.

3 Irrevocable Confirmed Credit. Should the UK bank be in a position to add its confirmation to the credit (and this is not necessarily a foregone conclusion) then the exporter has that bank's guarantee that, provided all conditions of the credit are fulfilled, payment will be made irrespective of what might happen to the opening bank or indeed the originating country. Maximum security of payment is gained by having a credit confirmed in this way, but the ability to confirm depends on the credit line the advising bank is prepared to extend to the opening bank. In some instances, in Iran a UK bank would be precluded from adding its confirmation by the Iranian authorities themselves.

These then are the basic types of credit available to you. As you become involved in exporting you will hear of other variations designed to meet specific purposes and which include Transferable Credits, Revolving Credits, Standby Credits, and so on. Any of these may be appropriate to your particular needs, and you should make early contact with your own bank for further details. Along with their other publications on exporting, most banks supply comprehensive booklets on documentary credits. These are highly recommended as a sound source of reference.

Whatever form of credit you encounter the general rules are the same. The first point to appreciate is that the paying bank has a mandate to pay, if the documents are in order and the terms and conditions are complied with precisely. Regrettably, over 50 per cent of credits cannot be paid on first presentation due to discrepancies. Many of these could easily be avoided by the beneficiary adopting a disciplined approach to his presentation procedure.

Prior to a documentary credit being established, the buyer and seller enter into a Contract of Sale which includes:

1 The price basis – reflecting terms of delivery, CIF, FOB, and so on (see Glossary).

Getting Paid

2 A period of time to allow for shipment by the seller and a latest date of shipment.
3 A description of the goods.
4 The method of payment agreed, ie by Documentary Credit payable in sterling at sight in London.
5 The method of despatch of the goods.
6 The documents required by the buyer.
7 The name of an arbitrator (in case of need) in the event of a dispute.
8 The name of the seller's bank through which the credit is to be advised/confirmed.
9 Details of who is to be responsible for paying bank charges, both at home and abroad.

If all these points are considered at the outset and the Contract of Sale is agreed between the parties, then a workable credit acceptable to the seller should result. It is as well to incorporate a date by which the credit is to be received, as this will enable you to alter prices, and so on, should the credit not be opened in a reasonable time.

When the credit is received, study the terms and conditions carefully and show it to your forwarding agent to ensure he can arrange the necessary shipping space. If you are unhappy with any aspect of the credit, seek clarification from the advising bank. If you know you are unable to comply with any requirement, request an immediate amendment from the buyer. You are now ready to ship the goods and present your documents to the advising bank for payment.

There are a number of documents basic to most credits and there may be additional ones relative to the goods you are exporting, or the country for which your goods are destined. The most important documents are listed below:

1 Documents evidencing movement of the goods. Depending on the mode of transport agreed, these may take the form of Bills of Lading, Air Waybills, Railway Consignment notes, Parcel Post Receipts, and so on. In other words, evidence that the goods have been released to a carrier for onward movement overseas.

2 Invoices. Commercial invoices will be required in the number of copies specified, giving a full description of the goods, the price, the terms of shipment, freight and insurance costs where payable, details of import licences and shipping marks as they appear on the movement document. A certified invoice or Certificate of Origin may be called for on which it will be necessary to certify the country of origin of the goods. The credit may call for this certification to be given by an approved Chamber of Commerce. Consular Invoices are required by some countries which usually take the form of specially printed documents available from the appropriate consulate, which have to be legalised. Delays can be encountered in obtaining legalised invoices, so early action is recommended when these are needed. Some consulates charge quite high fees for this service, another factor to be taken into account when setting your selling price.

3 Insurance certificates. It is essential that all goods for export are covered by insurance at every stage of the journey. Who is to pay for this insurance will have been agreed in the Contract of Sale.

Where insurance is arranged by the exporter, the credit will call for evidence to this effect, usually in the form of a Certificate of Insurance. It is also likely that the credit will call for a value at least 10 per cent over the invoice value. The risks covered should be exactly those stipulated, the certificate should not be dated after shipment, and if claims are payable at a specific place, then this too must be incorporated. These documents should also show the relative shipping marks for identification purposes.

4 Other documents. Depending on the type of goods being exported, the credit may also call for packing lists, weight notes, Certificates of Chemical Analysis, Health Certificates and the like, all of which are self-explanatory. Some foreign governments require all imports to be covered by a Clean Report of Findings given by an independent inspection agency. These agencies are established worldwide and will carry out a check on your own premises, prior to shipment, examining quality and quantity and making a price comparison. Make an early request for a visit, as there can be delays. This requirement is most common when exporting to African States.

'Blacklist Certificates' are called for by a number of countries requiring evidence that goods do not originate from

Getting Paid

a particular country with whom their relations are strained. They may also require statements regarding the registration of the carrying vessel and a guarantee that the vessel will not call at unfriendly ports.

These then are some of the documents you might be called upon to present. It is usual for the presentation to be accompanied by a Bill of Exchange. This is 'An unconditional order in writing addressed by one person (the drawer) to another (the drawee) signed by the person giving it, requiring the drawee to pay on demand, or at a fixed or determinable future time, a sum certain in money to, or to the order of a specified person, or to bearer'. A specimen Bill of Exchange can be found in Appendix I.

Once you have shipped the goods and prepared your documents, you should now present them as quickly as possible to the advising bank for payment. Your covering letter should:

1 List the documents enclosed.
2 Include the Documentary Credit reference number.
3 Clearly indicate how you wish to receive payment. It is normal practice for banks only to effect payment to the seller named in the credit.

On receiving the documents the bank will examine them and, if in order, payment will be made without recourse to the seller. Should the bank not be in a position to pay due to discrepancies which you cannot put right, they may offer three alternatives:

1 They may agree to pay against a bank indemnity. However, do remember that if your buyer does not eventually agree to accept the discrepancies, you will be called upon to reimburse the bank.

2 They may telex for permission to pay despite the listed discrepancies. If your buyer agrees, then the proceeds are paid irrevocably.

3 In the case of serious discrepancies, they may send out the documents 'In Trust' on a collection basis. Here you will have to wait until the documents are accepted by the buyer.

You can see, therefore, why it is so important that every effort is made to get the documents right first time.

Documentary Credits are issued subject to International Chamber of Commerce rules known as 'Uniform Customs and Practice for Documentary Credits'. It is advisable to obtain a copy of this publication so that you can understand the bank's interpretation of the rules.

Documentary Collection

If it is not possible for you to obtain a Documentary Letter of Credit from the overseas buyer, you can adopt the alternative method of sending the documents on a collection basis. Here, the shipping documents, including the Bills of Lading and other transport documents, are handed to your bank, which then sends them to a suitable bank in the buyer's country. Your buyer will then be notified of the arrival of these documents and the terms on which they will be released to him.

Depending on the terms of the sale you agreed originally, the Bill of Exchange may be drawn on the overseas buyer 'at sight'. This means that the documents will only be released to the buyer against payment of the bill. When documents of title are being set out, this 'documents against payment' procedure usually ensures that control over the goods is maintained by you until payment is made. However, there is always the risk that you will incur demurrage (or storage) charges and additional insurance costs should the bill not be paid promptly and the goods remain uncollected.

When your buyer's integrity is proved to be satisfactory you can then consider offering extended credit terms. In this case a 'Term Bill' may be drawn, calling for payment 30, 60, 90 or even 180 days after sight (or, in some cases, after date of shipment). Documents of title (ie proof of ownership) will be released following the buyer's acceptance of the bill. He is then able to take possession of the goods which then pass out of your control.

It should be noted that where the goods are despatched by airfreight or parcel post direct to the buyer, control of the goods is lost immediately on despatch.

Banks in the UK and in the majority of other countries, handle collections under the terms of the ICC 'Uniform Rules for Collections'. You can obtain a copy of these rules from The International Chamber of Commerce (see Appendix IV for the address).

One popular misconception with regard to Documentary Collections is that the overseas bank can enforce payment, or that they have earmarked funds to meet maturing Bills of Exchange. This is not so and the local bank can only follow instructions given by the remitting bank. One of these instructions may be to 'protest' the bill is unpaid at maturity, in which case the overseas bank will be required to instruct a Notary Public to make an official protest. He will call on the buyer and note the reason for non-payment on a 'Deed of Protest' and this, together with the dishonoured bill, form the basis for taking the matter to litigation. This is as far as the overseas bank can go, however, if the bill still remains unpaid, they will either arrange to return the goods to you or release them to your local agent, perhaps for sale to a different buyer.

Open Account

If you know you are dealing with a buyer of impeccable reputation, business can be conducted on an open account basis. In other instances competitive pressures within the market may make this a necessity.

In this case the simplest method of obtaining payment is to send any relevant documents to your customer for immediate payment, or for payment at a specified time. The customer may pay with his own cheque, but remember it is your company that will have to pay bank collection charges and take the risk of delay or even non-payment. For example, the cheque could be returned as a result of some technical irregularity as well as through lack of funds. These risks do need careful consideration. The overseas legal procedures required to enforce payment under an open account arrangement are more complicated than those to enforce payment of a bill for collection.

In order to avoid potential problems you can ask your customer to arrange for payment to be made either by banker's draft, or directly through their bank by means of a mail or cable transfer to the credit of your company's account. It is worth remembering that postal delays can occur and the expense of a cable transfer may well be worthwhile. Early receipt of funds can make a substantial contribution to your cashflow. Payment remitted in this way is by far the quickest and most effective method. To simplify such transfers, you would be well advised to quote the name and address of your bank together with your account number on the invoice.

Which Currency?

These then are the various methods of payment you are likely to encounter. We now need to move on to another important question – in what currency will you be paid?

Historically, UK exporters invoiced in sterling thus transferring the risk of adverse changes in the exchange rate to their customers. This situation has changed, in part due to the greater volatility of exchange rates in recent years. Quoting in sterling can also place you at a disadvantage if your competitors are quoting in the customer's preferred currency, whether his own or a third currency such as US dollars. Do remember to check first, however, that there is a market in the currency in which you are being asked to deal.

The risk you then run is that the exchange rate agreed at the time the order was placed will have changed adversely by the time the proceeds of the sale are received. You could take a chance and sell the currency at 'spot' (the rate ruling on the day) hoping it might be to your advantage. However, as a prudent exporter who is aware of the risks involved, you will consider ways in which you can crystallize your exchange risk at the outset. There are three ways this might be achieved, first by using currency accounts, second by selling the currency 'forward' or, third, by borrowing the currency in anticipation of receiving it in due course. Let us now consider each of these in more detail.

1 *Currency accounts* These are particularly useful where there is regular two-way flow in a given currency. For example, you might be buying raw materials from the same country to which you are selling finished goods.

The exchange risk is avoided, therefore, on currency you can hedge in this way. Such accounts can be maintained at your local bank and can take the form of a current account with cheque book, or alternatively an interest-bearing account. Let your branch manager know exactly what you wish to achieve with your currency account and he will advise the most appropriate type for your purpose.

2 *The Forward Exchange Contract* This is a legally

binding agreement between your company and the bank, to the effect that one currency will be exchanged for another at some future time, at a rate of exchange agreed upon at the time the contract is arranged. The rate is therefore guaranteed no matter what outside influence might affect the market. This means, of course, that you will be able to predict precisely the sum you will receive. Forward rates are arrived at by an adjustment to the spot rate, which mainly reflects the difference in interest rates between the two currencies. Hence a currency with a lower interest rate than sterling will usually be at a premium against sterling on the forward market, whilst a currency with a higher interest rate will be at a discount. Premiums are deducted from the spot rate and discounts are added to it.

Consequently, if you are selling in a currency which commands a premium and approach your bank with a view to selling that currency for sterling, at a date in the future corresponding to the expected date of receipt of the payment, you will be quoted a lower rate than the existing spot rate. Conversely, if the currency is sold at a discount, then the forward rate will be higher than the spot rate. Forward contracts can be arranged to mature at a given date in the future, but it is far from easy to predict that payment from your customer will arrive on that given date.

The alternative is to take out an option contract. This would enable you to deliver the currency at any time between the date of the contract and the maturity date, but this would preclude you from taking advantage of any premium involved. Therefore it is usually better in practice to take a limited option. This involves agreeing to sell the currency during a period of say one month, some six months ahead or, the approximate time you expect to be paid. In this way you will obtain the maximum benefit from any premium, but you will also retain some flexibility in utilising the contract.

3 *Foreign Currency Borrowing* The third means of minimising exchange risks may be to borrow a sum of currency from your bank in anticipation of receiving your export proceeds at a later date.

The currency so borrowed could be exchanged for sterling on the same day (spot rate), thus fixing your exchange rate. The resulting sterling sum could then be utilised to reduce your sterling borrowing. As currency proceeds are received they can be applied to the currency overdraft and interest will be charged appropriate to the currency you are borrowing. The effect of this is very similar to entering into a forward contract, as the advantage gained from a lower interest rate being applied to the overdraft would roughly equate to the premium obtained on a forward contract.

You can see, therefore, that while there can be advantages to selling in currency, there can also be risks. Being aware of these risks is the most important first step. The second step is to talk to your bank to see how best they can be minimised.

Arranging Finance

Let us now move on to look at the various options open to you for financing your export sales. The time lapse between purchasing raw materials needed to manufacture your product and actually getting paid for finished goods is an important part of your cost equation. Do not forget to include it in your calculations when arriving at your export price.

The most straightforward, and usually the cheapest means of finance, is through a bank overdraft. However, there are a wide range of services provided by banks to assist you with post-shipment finance. It is certainly a good idea to look at them all to ensure you select the one best suited to your company's circumstances.

Most banks have schemes specifically aimed at the smaller exporter. These provide limited recourse finance and also incorporate an element of credit insurance. Talk to your bank manager. Tell him what you are doing, which countries are involved, the methods of payment agreed and credit terms extended to your customers and the amounts involved in each transaction. He will need to have this information in order to assess your situation and guide you to the scheme most appropriate to your company's needs.

So, in conclusion:

1 Look to achieve the most secure method of payment you can, always bearing in mind the need to remain competitive.

2 Ensure that all the necessary members of your staff understand what they have to do with Letters of Credit. Emphasise that documents must be scrupulously checked against the credit before they are presented for payment.

Getting Paid

3 Be flexible when it comes to arranging whether payment is made in sterling or another suitable currency. Remember, there are added financial advantages, in the form of a premium, if you are paid in a strong currency and then sell it forward.

4 Ask your bank manager how best he can help you with finance for your exports.

Finally, do not take chances with orders which come out of the blue promising high profits. Always bear in mind that not everyone is as honest as you and that greed has proved the undoing of many a new and inexperienced exporter in the past.

6
Cargo Insurance

Although this is usually thought of, in common with most other areas of insurance, as being a highly complicated subject it is, in fact, relatively straightforward in most respects. As an exporter, it is important that you have at least a good working knowledge of the topic in order to protect the interests of both your company and your customer. Where the sale is agreed on a cash with order, ex-works basis you have no need to worry, but if any other terms are agreed then you should be aware of the problems which can occur.

Your Liabilities

As you are already aware, one of the most common methods of payment is by Letter of Credit, this is a document which gives specific instructions with which you must comply strictly in order to receive payment. Such instructions are normally laid out in various clauses, one of which will undoubtedly deal with the question of insurance. Here we are assuming that this will be a Cost, Insurance, Freight (CIF) Letter of Credit. The insurance clause will usually contain the conditions on which insurance must be placed (ie policy or certificate in duplicate) and will go on to state various specific risks which need to be covered, eg oil or water damage, and so on.

Since it is vital that the insurance documentation does comply completely with the insurance terms of the credit, it is essential that your insurer is supplied with a copy of the Letter of Credit. If they are not, there is a strong possibility that the two documents will not be compatible and that the bank concerned will refuse to accept them.

There are, however, some 36 countries, plus a number of Communist countries which have legislation of one form or another prohibiting the exporter from selling on CIF terms. If you are dealing with any of these countries and payment is to be made on a Confirmed Irrevocable Letter of Credit then once your products are onboard ship in good order and you have received payment, you are no longer in a position of risk. It is essential though, that you have adequate insurance cover until you reach this happy position. If you do not, and loss or damage occurs before the goods are safely loaded onboard the overseas vessel, you would be responsible for rectifying the situation.

Two other situations could also arise, where risk would revert back to you, the seller. Your buyer may refuse to accept the goods because they are damaged or you might have to exercise your right of *'stoppage in transitu'* if some unforeseen problem occurs. Two questions arise in situations like this. How can I protect myself if the buyer fails to insure (which can happen with Middle East destinations in particular)? Can I have the protection of the buyer's policy if he has in fact insured? The answer to the second question is invariably 'no'. In the case of the first question protection is available in the form of Sellers' Interest Contingency cover. This can be effected as cover on its own or can be an extension added to your standard Marine Open cover. The extension can be effected to include specific countries only, and as these would normally be the ones where the risk is highest, the premium is expensive. Alternatively, and as is more usual, it can cover all destinations and transactions where you are selling on Free on Board (FOB) or Cost & Freight (C&F) terms and where a letter of credit is not involved.

This is not 'double' insurance as may appear on the face of it. You, the seller, are merely buying a facility so that if the goods revert back to your responsibility at any time during transit — even if they are already lost or damaged — the underwriters agree to issue a full Warehouse to Warehouse Policy in your name. This will cover the goods from your warehouse and will be charged at normal policy rates of premium stated in the cover, less the premium already paid on your original declaration in respect of that particular shipment. You can then, if necessary, extend the cover until such time as your goods are either resold and delivered to the new customer, or are brought back to your own premises in the UK.

Unless there is specific agreement in your Contract of Sale

to the opposite effect, it is your responsibility to care for the goods until they are actually placed on board the carrying vessel. This rule applies under both FOB and C&F terms of sale. If loss or damage occurred prior to this point, you would have to make good the loss and then look to your insurers for reimbursement. It is essential, therefore, that all contracts are declared and the proper premium paid. Many exporters fail to include C&F contracts in their declarations on the assumption, often false, that their buyer in electing to insure the goods will have done so on a warehouse-to-warehouse basis. The buyer normally has no insurable interest until the goods are on board the vessel, and without prior agreement it is unlikely that their underwriters will accept liability. As a consequence, it is essential that you have your interests protected under the terms of your own insurance policy.

Even where local legislation requires that insurance be placed in the buyer's country, your buyer may still accept CIF terms if they are offered. This can lead to all kinds of problems for the exporter. He will find himself having to obtain an insurance certificate or policy either from a company resident and authorised to conduct business in the country of destination, or from the appropriate government department. Sometimes the difficulties created prove to be insurmountable. Rates charged are very often higher than in the UK, leading to greatly reduced profit margins where CIF prices have been quoted based on UK rates. The country concerned may also have currency regulations forbidding the transfer of any claims monies. You may even find it impossible to approach the foreign insurer direct, in which case your buyer will have to effect insurance on your behalf on a separate charge basis.

The only safe answer is to check with your insurers to discover if there are any regulations concerning insurance in the country where you are intending to trade, before concluding any contracts. Also ensure that your overseas sales representative, where applicable, fully understands the position as well.

The Carrier's Liabilities

The carrier, of course, also has certain obligations under the law with regard to your goods whilst they are in his possession. By its very nature, the transport industry involves custodianship of goods during loading, carriage and delivery, and common law requires that the carriers exercise a reasonable amount of custodial care and take reasonable steps to ensure the safety of the goods carried. This common law requirement covers road and rail carriers, freight forwarders, warehouse keepers, shipowners and airlines. Responsibility can be altered by contract but such a contract would have to be fair to all parties in accordance with the conditions of the Unfair Contracts Bill.

In order to avoid the need for litigation the various governing bodies, such as the Road Haulage Association (RHA), the Institute of Freight Forwarders (IFF) and the National Association of Warehouse Keepers (NAWK), drew up their own contract conditions in conjunction with their legal advisers. These conditions introduced a degree of stability into the market-place and gave a basis upon which individual contracts could be built. They state the liabilities which the carrier is content to bear and those which he is not. Also they stipulate the maximum monetary amount the carrier would be prepared to pay in compensation under such liability. However, there is one set of conditions which apply to international road hauliers and which supersede all others. They are known as the CMR Convention Conditions and were ratified in English law by the Carriage of Goods by Road Act 1965.

Rail carriers, such as British Rail and the Post Office, have their own conditions of carriage for both domestic and international routes. In the case of air carriers, they are subject to the rules of the Warsaw Convention.

The conditions affecting shipowners are different in that they are laid down by the Carriage of Goods by Sea Act 1971. These are known as the Hague Visby Rules and they apply to all outward Bills of Lading from the UK and inward bills from other signatories to the Rules. Most other bills, coming from non-signatory countries, will be subject to the earlier Hague Rules.

As a businessperson you will be very aware of the need to read the small print in any contract very carefully. In the case of insurance contracts this is of paramount importance. You need to be aware from the outset exactly what contingencies the policy covers and, just as important, those which it does not. This applies equally when dealing with transporters. Be sure you known precisely the extent of their liability cover and ensure that your own policy covers any areas which theirs does not.

Making a Claim

What action do you then need to take if, having done everything correctly, you suffer some loss or damage? Marine Insurance requires that you, the claimant, must prove your claim to the insurer by providing proof that:

1   The goods were insured.
2   The goods were despatched.
3   Loss or damage has been suffered.
4   The cause of the loss or damage and that it occurred during the policy period.

All such evidence must be independent and documentary and supplied to the underwriter as quickly as possible, if delay in settlement is to be avoided.

At the time of the loss you, the claimant, must have an insurable interest in the goods, and the first action you must take is to make a reservation against the carrier concerned within the time limit specified by the conditions of carriage. The insurer, or his agent, in the country of destination stated in the policy must then be notified (verbally and in writing) of the possible claim and their advice followed. Where damage to the goods has taken place, a surveyor must be appointed to assess the loss and act as an independent witness, submitting a detailed report. You must then present the insurer with a full set of supporting documents in evidence of your claim.

This claim must include:

1   A quantified statement of the loss.

2   A copy of the commercial invoice giving full details of the value of the consignment. This will also establish ownership of the goods.

3   An original Bill of Lading to prove the goods were shipped and, where applicable, the state in which they were received by the shippers.

4   A delivery note which will indicate the condition of the goods upon despatch from the carrier. In the case of both

domestic and international road transport this may be the only transit document available.

5   The original certificate or policy of insurance to prove the goods were insured.

6   In the case of damage, the survey report to provide independent evidence that damage has been sustained and to give some indication of how that damage occurred.

7   In the case of non-delivery or partial non-delivery of the consignment by road, your written claim on the carrier together with evidence of their inability to prove delivery.

All correspondence with the carrier regarding the loss or damage must be submitted to your underwriter who, on payment of the claim to you, will take over all rights against the carrier. Upon settlement of your claim the underwriter will usually require you to sign a Letter of Subrogation. This acknowledges receipt of the claim and transfers your rights against third parties to him, whilst agreeing to assist him in his pursuit of the claim against the carrier.

This chapter will have given you an outline of the things to look for when arranging export insurance as well as some idea of the pitfalls and problems which can arise on a day-to-day basis. It will also have made you aware how important it is to build up a good working relationship with your broker/underwriter, so that he is fully aware of your company's ongoing requirements. This will enable him to get the cover required to meet all potential risks at the best possible price.

7

Methods of Transport

When negotiating your export sales contract the method of transport to be used in getting the product from your company to the customer will need to be decided upon at an early stage. Not only will these costs need to be taken into consideration when arriving at the selling price you quote to your customer, but cargo space will have to be booked and the appropriate documentation prepared. You will also need to consider the type of packing to be used, the cost of which can vary considerably. For example, it is pointless using expensive wooden-case packing if, for instance, the goods are to be transported on a door-to-door basis by express van without any intermediate handling.

In some cases the mode of transport to be used will be determined by the terms of sale you finally negotiate. Many British exporters today still sell on traditional terms, ie FOB or ex-works. As a newcomer to exporting, do not fall into this trap. Look at the alternatives which are available and choose the one that is in the best interests of your company, whilst allowing you to remain competitive.

The standard terms used in selling exports are known as *Incoterms*. They are defined and published by the International Chamber of Commerce from their London Office (see Appendix IV for their full address). The Swedish Freight Forwarders Association produces a publication called *Combiterms* which lays out clearly a definition of the payment responsibilities of both buyer and seller in an export contract. The Association's full address can be found in Appendix IV. Also, in the Glossary, you will find a list of the most commonly used terms (eg FOB, CIF, C&F and so on) and a short definition of your responsibilities with regard to each.

The next point you will need to consider is the time available for shipment. This will, of course, be a primary consideration in selecting the mode of transport to be used. As a general rule, the shorter the available transit time the more expensive the cost is likely to be. Obviously there are other factors which also need to be taken into account:

1 The cost of financing the goods while in transit.

2 The relative packing costs for different methods of transport.

3 Storage costs prior to despatch.

4 Penalty clauses for late delivery.

5 The type of goods being shipped and any special regulations pertaining to them. For example are the goods perishable, do they come under the regulations for dangerous goods, are they particularly fragile or prone to damage from excess heat or cold?

Let us now examine the four principal methods of transport traditionally available to the British exporter.

Air

According to the most up-to-date statistics available, some 70 per cent of air freight carried by scheduled airlines is tendered to them through the medium of air freight forwarders. Most of this air freight is carried in the cargo holds of scheduled services. Interestingly, without the revenue derived from freight most passenger air services would not be financially viable. Air freight shipment can be roughly divided into three categories – direct airline bookings, consolidations, and charter or part charter.

Direct airline bookings

When moving cargo under the first system, the air freight forwarder or shipper books space direct with the airline. This is then moved on the first available, or nominated flight at a tariff rate published by the International Air Transport Association (IATA). This is normally the fastest, and consequently the most expensive method of moving freight by air.

Methods of Transport

The documentation issued to cover this airport-to-airport movement is the Air Waybill (AWB). This bill has a unique identifying number which is used to track the consignment throughout its transit.

Consolidations

Under the consolidation system, the air freight forwarder groups together a number of shipments from different clients. These are then offered to the airline as one large shipment, nowadays often as a container load. By doing so he is able to obtain lower freight rates and some of this benefit can then be passed back to the individual customers. The overall transit time is normally slightly longer than when using direct IATA shipments. This is because, dependent on the ultimate destination, departure will not necessarily be on a daily basis. It will often depend on the overall cargo density of the route and the consolidator's share of the market.

Freight rates will reflect this slightly extended timescale and can show a significant saving on the IATA costs. The document issued to cover such a consolidation service is the House Airway Bill (HAWB) of the freight forwarder you use.

(Note that AWBs and HAWBs are *not* title documents, and to be certain of securing payment you should consign your goods to a bank in the country of destination).

Charter

The third division of freight by air, is charter or part charter. It is unlikely, however, that a company new to exporting would be concerned with this method since it involves chartering either a whole cargo plane, or part of one, for a given flight. Therefore, this is only a viable method of transport where very large shipments are concerned.

Road

Road represents the principal method of transport between the UK and continental Europe, including Scandinavia. The cross-Channel or North Sea leg of the journey is an integral part of the service offered by the road haulier, who provides a door-to-door or depot-to-depot service, as appropriate. The sea journey is normally achieved by shipping either the trailer alone, or the trailer plus cab and driver, on a roll on/roll off (ro/ro) ship between the British and Continental ports.

How to Export

Shipments by road can be divided into two main categories, full load and part load or groupage. As a general rule, you can consider a full-load movement when you have a shipment comprising of 15 to 16 tonnes in weight and/or 45 to 50 cubic metres in capacity. If your shipment is only slightly smaller than this, the haulier may agree to collect the freight in the vehicle undertaking the international journey, thus eliminating the need for intermediate handling. Small consignments, however, will have to be moved to a central depot where sufficient cargo to make up a complete trailer load will be assembled.

Tariffs

There are no mandatory tariffs for international road transport services from the UK. You will need to negotiate them with the haulier and it pays to 'shop around' and find the best deal. Do remember though that the lowest price is not necessarily the main criterion – the quality of service offered is equally important. Your overseas customer is only interested in receiving his order on time and in good condition. Rates for full-load movements can be negotiated and are generally based on a lump sum door-to-door basis, with no hidden extras.

Most hauliers operating trailer groupage services publish their own tariffs. These are based on final destination city, area or country, together with details of their receiving depots in the UK. Rates are issued on a Freight-All-Kinds (FAK) per tonne basis, with the cost per tonne decreasing in proportion to the increasing size of the consignment. As with air consolidation, departure frequency depends on the destination involved. This would usually be at least weekly, but in many instances to the more popular destinations can be up to three or four times a week.

There are a large number of hauliers serving the principal markets of Europe, namely France, Germany, Benelux, Austria, Switzerland and Italy. A smaller number specialise in the Scandinavian market and even fewer in the Eastern Bloc and Middle Eastern countries. The overland route to the Middle East has declined in popularity due to both the political instability of certain areas en route and the improved performance of the ports in the area.

Some keen rates can be obtained from foreign hauliers looking for return loads for their vehicles because of the

Methods of Transport

imbalance between the level of British imports and exports. However, the problems which can face the exporter when selecting a reliable haulage company are dealt with in more detail later in this chapter.

The documentation issued to cover an international movement by road is known as the CMR Note. This is a Waybill issued by the haulier giving details of the consignment, the contract of carriage and the terms and conditions under which the contract is to be executed. The international agreement covering this is known as the CMR Convention, which applies in 24 countries.

Rail

In the main the movement of UK exports to Europe by rail is confined to large and regular flows of traffic and, as such, is not likely to be of interest to the majority of new exporters. There are, however, still a small number of freight forwarders who operate groupage services to Europe by rail. The services they offer will be largely similar to those of the road-based operators outlined in the previous section. The projected Channel Tunnel, should it finally be built, will add a whole new dimension to this area of cargo movement. Once open and fully operational it will, for the first time ever, offer rail the opportunity to compete with road on a cost and transit time basis.

In addition to the traditional rail ferry wagon, designed to run on both British and Continental railways, there will undoubtedly be door-to-door container services using block trains between the despatch and destination points. This service will afford transit times as competitive as any offered by road hauliers. The introduction of a fixed link across the Channel could, therefore, radically alter the existing balance of freight movement between road and rail.

As with road transport, there is an international document covering transport by rail throughout Europe. It is known as the CIM Note and is effectively a rail Waybill.

Sea

Within this area of cargo transport, deep-sea markets are generally defined as lying east of Suez or across the Atlantic. However, the following principles are the same for North Africa and the Eastern Mediterranean.

As a result of the container revolution of the late 1960s, it is virtually certain that your cargo will leave the UK in a container. As with road haulage the type of operation will depend on the size of the consignment. In deep-sea shipping, measurement is more critical than weight and a consignment of about 16 to 18 cubic metres would be required to justify the exclusive use of a container, although this figure may be higher in certain trades.

Shipping lines may be divided roughly into two categories, Conference and non-Conference (independent) lines.

Conference Lines

Conferences are made up of a number of independent lines which have banded together, separately or as a consortia, to provide regular, frequent departures and reliable transit times to a wide range of ports in the area which they serve. They are also likely to be able to offer a wide selection of specialised container equipment.

Non-Conference Lines

As the name suggests, independent lines operate as individual companies. They tend to have more flexibility in the rate-making process, but may not serve as wide a range of ports as the conference lines, nor have available as wide a range of specialised container equipment. However, it is no longer true to say that independent lines lack the financial resources of conference carriers, as used to be implied.

Tariffs

Freight tariffs for Full Container Load (FCL) shipments are generally quoted in US dollars per container, on a port-to-port basis, depending on commodity. You can also obtain a door-to-door rate from the carrier which will include elements for inland haulage, port handling, ocean freight, destination port handling and final delivery to your customer. Surcharges are still common in deep-sea shipping. The most frequently used are Currency Adjustment Factor (CAF) and Bunker Adjustment Factor (BAF). These are sometimes computed together and shown as CABAF.

Arranging a full container load shipment is simple. You merely have to telephone or telex the selected carrier or forwarder, giving details of the shipment, and the time and

Methods of Transport

place of loading. Each shipment must be accompanied by a Standard Shipping Note (see Appendix I for example).

The shipment of a part-container load, also known as Less-than-Container Load (LCL) or groupage, follows the same pattern as air or European road consolidation. The actual consolidator or groupage operator may be the shipping line itself or a separate freight forwarder, but the principle of operation is the same for both. LCL cargo is delivered into a receiving depot, of which there are a large number throughout the country. Here it is made up into full container loads and shipped to a similar depot in the destination country. Upon arrival the container is stripped and its cargo made available for custom's clearance and delivery.

The rate basis is becoming increasingly simpler and comprises a cost, usually in US dollars, which covers depot-to-depot movement. This is normally quoted per freight ton, ie per cubic metre or tonne whichever is the greater. To this is added additional charges for the various other elements carried out by the operator, eg collection, depot handling, documentation, and so on. Today many forwarders, when acting as consolidators, will rate LCL shipments on a FAK basis, and some conference lines are also now following this lead.

The principal document used in ocean shipping is the Bill of Lading (see Appendix I for sample). This is a negotiable document, in other words a document of title to the goods specified thereon. The equivalent document issued by a forwarder when acting as a carrier is the FIATA FBL, which is now accepted by banks worldwide under the Documentary Credit Rules of the International Chamber of Commerce (ICC). Bills of Lading are normally issued in two or three original copies and are used in effecting payment for the goods through the banking system, and also as authority for the release of goods at their destination.

The FBL is a combined transport Bill of Lading and can, therefore, cover all the separate legs of a through transport movement, irrespective of the mode of transport used for any given sector. Consequently you, the exporter, only have to deal with one company in the event of a claim or liability problem. When a document of title is not required, for example where you have received payment in advance for your goods, the Bill of Lading may be replaced by the Waybill. This provides evidence of shipment of goods and can avoid potential delays at the destination should a negotiable document be lost or delayed.

Freight Forwarders

As a new exporter, the best place for you to turn for assistance is undoubtedly the freight forwarder. Forwarding companies come in many types and sizes, from large multinational organisations, with branches throughout the world, to the small specialist with half a dozen staff. The most useful guide for the new exporter in choosing a suitable freight forwarder is to ensure that it is registered with the Institute of Freight Forwarders. Through the Institute's registration scheme each company meeting the IFF's requirements is allocated a registration number. They are then authorised to display this number, together with the IFF logo, on their letterheads and when advertising.

A freight forwarder, acting as your agent, will undertake all the responsibilities associated with international transport. These include a selection of a suitable carrier, preparation of documentation (including legalisation and presentation to banks), packing and cargo supervision if required. Many operate their own services, for example as air freight consolidators, European road hauliers and deep-sea groupage operators. They have their own cargo receiving depots located throughout the country, and operate fleets of collection and delivery vehicles. Today the larger groups are investing heavily in computers and electronic data interchange capability. This investment augments the range of services which they provide by improved documentation procedures and facilitates cargo tracking on a worldwide scale.

You would be well advised to develop a close working relationship with your forwarding agent. The more he knows about your business and aspirations in the export market, the better will be the advice he is able to give you. Full details of registered forwarders in the UK and the specialised services they provide can be obtained from the Institute of Freight Forwarders (full address can be found in Appendix IV).

8

Documentation

In the minds of everyone who initially contemplates the idea of taking a company into the export market, the most daunting thought is not that of having to research the market-place, find suitable outlets for goods or services or negotiate with potential customers. It is the thought of all the complicated paperwork which appears to be necessary to ensure the swift, safe movement of goods across national boundaries. Nothing increases costs and displeases customers so much as a delivery which is held up because arrangements have not been properly planned and the correct paperwork provided. This axiom applies even more so when exporting.

If you really want to export successfully, then these matters need to be treated as part of your total marketing exercise from day one of your preparations. To treat them as an afterthought is a mistake which could undo all the hard work you have done in researching the market, getting your product right and convincing the overseas buyer that he should buy from you rather than anyone else. Remember, you do not have a satisfied customer until the order is actually in his hands, in good condition. Equally, it is pointless obtaining overseas orders if you do not receive settlement of your account on time and in a suitable currency.

Once you have secured the order and written confirmation has been received from the overseas customer, you need to make sure that everyone within your company who will be involved in fulfilling that order is fully briefed.

You should also advise your customer, whether by letter, cable, telex or fax, that their order has been received, reiterating the precise details and confirming that terms and conditions are fully understood.

How to Export

The order will then have to be written into the production schedule and, if necessary, materials purchased. The packing department will need to be alerted to any special requirements, in particular the need to ensure that any packaging is clearly and correctly marked in line with the export documentation.

Having ensured that all the necessary steps have been taken to manufacture, inspect and pack the goods, you must also ensure that the correct export documentation is being prepared. If this is not done your goods could be held up and incur substantial costs thousands of miles away because of a simple error, omission or missing document.

The actual paperwork involved will, of course, vary depending on whether you elect to use a freight forwarder or undertake the task yourself. As already advised, unless you are in a position where you are exporting regularly and have the necessary experience, it is much wiser, safer and cheaper to use a freight forwarder – especially after January 1988 when the new Single Administrative Document (SAD) comes into force. However, should you decide to do it yourself, your local chamber of commerce can provide guidance as to which forms are needed and how to fill them in.

Alternatively, you may prefer to use the services of an export administration company which will attend to all the documentation on your behalf. These companies are usually quite small and act as your own export department, which will probably work out cheaper than the cost of your own time or that of your staff. Details of these companies can be obtained by contacting the Simplification of International Trade Procedures Board (SITPRO) whose full address is given in Appendix IV. SITPRO can also supply a comprehensive range of one-typing sets of export documents which can cut form filling and checking times considerably – also obtainable from SITPRO is an export documentation starter kit.

What forms will you normally have to supply?

An export invoice

Almost always you will have to supply several copies of your invoice (often up to eight). This invoice contains more information than normally found on a home trade invoice. In addition to the normal terms of credit and delivery terms, for

Documentation

example, an overseas invoice should state what the payment terms are, in what currency and taking what form. Also needed on a invoice going overseas are any special contractual terms and any additional information that is specific to the country to which you are exporting.

Each export invoice may also need to be individually signed by an authorised company signatory.

Check with your forwarder or Chamber of Commerce on the current requirements for this extra information in your own particular market, as these requirements often change. You should also allow additional time if this invoice needs to be certified by an official body, such as the embassy of the country to which you are exporting. Double check that what is entered on the invoice is *identical*, letter by letter, with the description of the goods where payment is to be by Letter of Credit.

Do not use codes, jargon or impenetrable technicalities when describing goods on export invoices. Clear descriptions in English and, if possible, the language of the customer's country will help avoid delays at customs and other points – queries often get put at the bottom of the pile!

Even if you are only sending sales literature or samples on a free-of-charge basis you must always supply an invoice. Such items must also be given a nominal value for customs purposes. A sample of a typical export invoice can be found in Appendix I.

Export Cargo Shipping Instructions

Clear instructions to your shipper can avoid problems at a later stage. Details given on this form must set out the information exactly as it appears in, say, the transport document. Be particularly careful where a Letter of Credit transaction is concerned. In fact, it is good practice to send a copy of the Letter of Credit to your forwarder immediately you receive it.

Special Documents

These are only required for a minority of exports and depend on:

1 Where the goods are going. For example, a special EUR 1 Movement Certificate for Scandinavia and some

other countries, and a Chamber of Commerce Certificate of Origin for a number of others. Some governments, especially in Africa, appoint an inspection agency to check prices and goods before shipment and issue the relevant paperwork. Take extra precautions with such transactions for without this agency's agreement to your prices, costings and exchange rates, as well as to the standard of your goods, you cannot obtain the necessary 'Clean report of findings'. This means you will be unable to obtain payment under a Letter of Credit, even if you and your customer are satisfied on all accounts.

2   The method of payment. If a Letter of Credit is involved, a variety of special documents may be called for and must be provided precisely correct. Do check on the day the Letter of Credit is received that they can all be provided on time. If presenting documents otherwise through a bank, say for the bank to hand over to the customer against payment, the appropriate collection form is required. Your bank will advise.

Other forms

Check in particular about any other requirements for your goods and markets, such as package marking or weights and measures, and any special customs treatment, for example, exemption from UK import duties on materials being processed into exports or origin regulations of importing countries. The BOTB are able to assist on such foreign regulations and *Croner's Exporters' Handbook* is a useful source of reference if you eventually expand your export operation to take in more than one market-place.

With guidance from your forwarder or local chamber of commerce on what forms are needed and how to fill them in, the job will appear much more straightforward than it seems at first sight. Remember that most UK exports need no more from exporters than suitable invoices and shipping instructions, including unrestricted products sent to anywhere in the EEC or North America.

As at 1 January 1988, an all-encompassing customs document has been produced and designed. This document is called the Single Administrative Document. In the following section we give further details on this new system but it would be advisable to obtain from HM Customs and Excise a copy of their book entitled *Single Administrative Document Customs freight procedures from 1 January 1988*.

Documentation

The Single Administrative Document

Previously goods moving between the UK and other EEC countries were normally the subject of three customs declarations, one each for export, transit and import purposes. Community Transit documents were standard throughout the EEC but import and export forms varied in each member state although the information they requested was very similar.

The need to simplify this documentation to facilitate trade and prepare for the computerised communication of customs data, has led to the development of the Single Administrative Document (SAD). This takes advantage of the similarities in information requirement throughout the EEC and can be used as an export, transit and import declaration for any consignment moving within the Community. In order to avoid unnecessary complexity, declarations for exports to and imports from non-Community countries will also be made on the same form. It will, therefore, replace most existing import, export and transit declarations for non-Community countries also.

There may be situations, of course, where use of a SAD to perform all three of its intended functions is not possible. In such cases it will be possible for separate copies of the forms for individual functions (export, import or transit) to be used instead.

This new system of forms started from 1 January 1988 and will be introduced in all EEC member states. It is advisable, therefore, to go to your local chamber of commerce and be thoroughly briefed as whilst there is a single document to fill in there are nine forms to choose from depending upon what you are exporting and where you are exporting to. Each of those nine forms is in turn printed on NCR paper. An example of the document can be found in Appendix I.

The following explanation as to what form goes where when stripped from its NCR duplicates is taken from the HM Customs and Excise book mentioned on page 88.

Copy 1 (Copy for the country of dispatch/export) remains at the office of departure for the purposes of control and may also be used for other export control purposes.

Copy 2 (Statistical copy – country of dispatch/export) is the copy of the export declaration for statistical purposes.

Copy 3 (Copy for the consignor/exporter) is the exporter's

or agent's copy or may be retained by the CT [Community Transit] principal.

Copy 4 (Copy for the office of destination) is for Customs in the member state of destination to act as evidence that the goods are (or are not) in free circulation (ie to indicate whether Customs duty is payable).

Copy 5 (Copy for return – CT) is returned from the office of destination to Customs in the member state of despatch to provide evidence that the goods have reached their destination intact.

Copy 6 (Copy for the country of destination) is used in the member state of destination as the customs import declaration on arrival.

Copy 7 (Statistical copy – country of destination) is the copy of the import declaration for statistical purposes in the member state of destination.

Copy 8 (Copy for the consignee) is for retention by the importer or his agent and, in the UK, will serve as the VAT copy for goods cleared at locations which are not served by the Customs computerised entry proceeding system (DEPS).

Copies 1 – 3, therefore, remain in the member state of dispatch, whilst copies 4 – 8 travel forward with the goods.

Once the form is signed by the person who is authorised by your company, then this commits the company to the facts entered on the form for export. If information is found to be incorrect then it must be amended and drawn to HM Customs and Excise's attention.

The SAD form is available from HM Customs and Excise. However, it may be printed privately provided that the form conforms to the official specimen and approval is granted. For details on how to obtain approval contact the Print Procurement Unit, GASD Branch 2A, HM Customs and Excise, King's Beam House, Mark Lane, London EC3R 7HE.

9
Case Studies

This book has been written not only to give you all the information you need to begin exporting with, but also to point out the potential problems which can arise. The following are case studies involving six of the most common problem areas which new – and sometimes even experienced – exporters can meet. They are all based on incidents which can and do happen, although the names given are purely fictitious. In all of the studies, the correct procedure to follow is obvious.

Case Study 1

ABC Plastics had been delighted to negotiate a contract to supply a major new hospital in Saudi Arabia with a wide range of plastic bowls and containers. These were to be shipped in containers from the UK to the nearest major port to the hospital site to await collection by the main contractors. The items were duly manufactured, inspected and packed in standard cardboard cartons, which were then loaded into a container for shipment.

Several weeks later the shipment arrived in Saudi Arabia and was unloaded onto the dock to await collection. The main contractor's trailer finally arrived four days later to pick up the container and take it to the hospital. During the four days on the dockside where temperatures inside the container had reached 60 to 70 degrees Centigrade the consignment sustained considerable damage. However, this was only found out when the container was eventually unloaded and the full scale of the disaster became apparent. As temperatures inside the container had built up, so the plastic had softened and the cardboard containers in which the items were packed had concertinaed downwards one into another. What remained was a misshapen heap of torn cardboard and distorted or melted plastic.

The whole consignment had to be scrapped and the suppliers were left with a very large bill for production and transport, which their insurers were unwilling to meet. More importantly, they also had an extremely irate customer who made it quite clear that they were unlikely to place any future orders with ABC Plastics.

After that incidence, all future orders being shipped overseas to countries where the temperatures exceed 20 degrees Centigrade had an immediate clearance order placed against them. This fact was clearly noted on the documentation and firm instructions sent to the shipping agents.

Case Study 2

Showerfit Limited was contacted by a Portuguese-based building consortium interested in negotiating a five-year contract to supply shower units and other bathroom accessories for a number of holiday complexes. Although this was potentially a very large order, their Sales Director, Alex Simmons was unable to fit a trip to Portugal into his already busy schedule. Since their only sales representative was away on holiday at the time, he decided that as long as everything was prepared beforehand, his assistant, David Coombes, could make the trip.

David arrived in Faro at the offices of the prospective customer, with the appropriate samples and quotation. The Portuguese buyer, who spoke excellent English, was impressed with the quality of the samples he was shown. However, he was not so happy with the prices quoted, asking for a further 5 per cent reduction. Unfortunately David, having been sent simply as a messenger, was not authorised to re-negotiate the quotation without prior permission from Alec Simmons. Alex was on a business trip to Scandinavia and so David was unable to speak with him until late the following evening. When they finally spoke, a further price reduction was agreed, despite the fact that it would cut into their tight profit margins. Alex then told David that he considered that the contract was important and could give Showerfit entry into a potentially lucrative market. He apologised for not briefing David properly beforehand.

Case Studies

First thing the next morning the Portuguese buyer telephoned David to explain that the contract had been awarded the previous afternoon to a major competitor. Their competitor's General Sales Manager had arrived in person to conduct the negotiations, had been able to make on-the-spot decisions and had, therefore, clinched the deal for his company. The buyer did tell David that the products' quality and delivery time were alike and that the deciding factor had been based on a speedy decision as to the final cost.

Case Study 3

As a medium-sized company manufacturing door hinges and seat ratchets for the motor industry, Williams and Sons decided to explore the possibility of selling their product to the US market. Extensive market research showed that sales opportunities were excellent, but that their current safety and quality tests – which more than satisfied UK and European regulations – fell somewhat short of those required by American law.

Meeting these very stringent requirements would mean re-writing test specifications, upgrading some existing test equipment and totally replacing others, re-training inspection personnel and re-planning existing production schedules to take all these factors into consideration. After lengthy and very detailed consultations, the Board made the decision to go ahead with the project. Their bank was able to provide the additional finance required. The detailed plans which were drawn up and implemented ensured minimum disruption to the existing workflow.

The results over the last 10 years have proven that the Board's decision was correct. Orders from the USA have increased year by year and the company is now considering the possibility of actually setting up its own manufacturing plant there. The Board has also worked on an option should the US market go into a decline so as to protect the company's financial position. Research on other overseas markets is due for implementation shortly.

Case Study 4

Medicheck, manufacturers of precision monitors for use in hospitals, had been exporting their products to a specialist importer in India for six months. Payment was always by Letter of Credit and to date matters had proceeded smoothly.

Towards the end of July, when the girl who usually dealt with the export invoices was on holiday, a consignment of 20 monitors became due for despatch. The temporary typist was merely told the number of units involved and to copy the rest of the details from the previous export invoice. The eight copies of the export invoice were hurriedly signed by the Sales Director en route to an important meeting with a major client. No one else in the department thought to check through the invoice.

The goods and paperwork were despatched by air to India and confirmation of receipt was duly received. Medicheck then presented the appropriate documentation to their customer's UK bank for payment via the Letter of Credit. They were horrified when four days later they received a letter advising them that payment could not be released, since the information on their invoice differed from that on the Letter of Credit.

Upon checking, it was found that the temporary typist had, as instructed, copied from an invoice on which monitor type HPM2a had been supplied. The current consignment had been of monitor type HPM2c – as correctly shown on the Letter of Credit.

It was only after several expensive telephone calls to India, followed up by confirmatory letters, that the matter was eventually sorted out and payment finally received some three months later.

Case Study 5

Whilst on a holiday in Florida, Alan Grey, owner of Mirrors Unlimited a small, specialist glass manufacturer, realised that there was a potential market for his expensive reproduction mirrors in selected outlets. At a party one night he was introduced to the Vice President of an exclusive firm of interior decorators, with 20 studios throughout the USA. He was due to visit Britain the next month and arrangements were made for him to call at Mirrors Unlimited for further discussions. The visit was successful and a three-year contract was agreed on the spot at a fixed price.

Over the next 12 months the level of export orders continued to rise. Eventually the factory's limited production facilities were so overstretched that even a minor stoppage or

Case Studies

breakdown on a machine presented a major problem. The continual need to try and meet the increased number of orders from America on time led to a serious backlog of domestic orders, with a consequent decline in customer relations.

This snap decision to export to the USA had originally been made without proper market research and planning. Alan Grey now found that his company was in a position where it had insufficient capacity to meet demand and additional overheads which had not been taken into account when prices had been agreed (eg special export packaging), cutting profit margins to a bare minimum. Also because it had been agreed that payment would be made in US dollars the company was faced with increased bank charges and, of course, the time taken to settle invoices was longer.

The outcome was that Mirrors Unlimited needed to expand by moving to larger premises and to raise sufficient finance to purchase the additional machinery and employ personnel required to meet increased order levels. Unfortunately, because of a total lack of forward planning and major cash flow problems, time ran out. The company's two main suppliers of raw materials refused to make any further deliveries until all overdue invoices were cleared.

Alan Grey was faced with two alternatives. He could either let his company go into liquidation, or to try to re-negotiate the American contract on more favourable terms. Because of the very strong demand for his product and the limited number of alternative suppliers he was, in fact, lucky enough to be able to re-negotiate the contract. On this basis the bank was able to arrange the additional funding he required to expand and prosper.

Case study 6

Over a number of years Hamish McLaren had gradually built up a good reputation with the UK as a geological surveyor, working mainly within the areas of water and coal prospecting.

Whilst attending a conference in London he met a senior civil servant from a French-speaking African country. Some time later he received a letter, in French, asking him to tender for a geological survey on a large agricultural project being funded by the UN.

Armed with a reasonable working knowledge of spoken French and an English/French dictionary he prepared his tender and despatched it by airmail to arrive well before the closure date. A couple of months passed and then one morning he received an official letter advising him that his tender had been accepted and requesting that he fly out to meet various government representatives to finalise details.

The visit was arranged, and he was courteously welcomed. It was only much later that he found out just how much amusement his tender had originally caused. Throughout it when talking about core samples he had, in fact, used the translation for an apple core! Luckily, in this instance, his amateur translation had not lost him business. However, many other companies who try to cut corners on professional translation costs have not been so fortunate.

These are only a few examples of the differences between domestic and export business and the problems involved. There are many other problems, of course, such as local customs, different business practices, exchange controls and so on. However, by ensuring that you carry out in-depth market research, initiate a detailed survey of your company's current resources and future requirements and obtain sound professional advice you can avoid potential problems.

All arrangements should be doubled checked, all those involved in exporting should be thoroughly briefed, even the simplest of procedures should never be overlooked or left to chance.

The markets are there. British goods and services are as much in demand now throughout the world as they were 50 or 100 years ago – even given the fact that there are far more competitors now than there were then. And even with fluctuating world markets, provided you have allowed for sufficient variation financially and in demand/supply, then there is no reason why you should not export successfully.

Appendix I

Samples of commonly used documents

How to Export

EXPORT INVOICE

	INVOICE	RECHNUNG FACTURA	FACTURE فاتورة
Seller (name, address, VAT reg. no.)

SITPRO
Simpler International Trade
Simplification of International Trade Procedures Board (SITPRO)
Almack House, 26/28 King Street, London SW1Y 6QW
Tel: 01-930 0532 Fax: 01-930 5779
Telex: 919130 SITPRO G. Prestel 20468
VAT Reg. No. 241 8235 77
SITPRO is a BOTB activity

© SITPRO 1987

Invoice number	
Invoice date (tax point)	Seller's reference
Buyer's reference	Other reference

Consignee

Buyer (if not consignee)

Country of origin of goods | Country of destination

Terms of delivery and payment

| Vessel/flight no. and date | Port/airport of loading |
| Port/airport of discharge | Place of delivery |

Shipping marks; container number | No. and kind of packages; description of goods | Commodity code | Total gross wt (kg) | Total cube (m³)

Total net wt (kg)

| Item/packages | Gross/net/cube | Description | Quantity | Unit price | Amount |

SPECIMEN

Invoice total

It is hereby certified that this invoice shows the actual price of the goods described, that no other invoice has been or will be issued, and that all particulars are true and correct.

Name of signatory

Place and date of issue

Signature

© SITPRO 1987 V5

(Reproduced by permission of SITPRO)

Appendix I

SHIPPING INSTRUCTIONS NOTE

(Reproduced by permission of SITPRO)

How to Export

BILL OF LADING

Consignor		FBL Number	Customs Reference/Status	GB
	FBL	Shipper's Reference		
		Forwarder's Reference		

Consigned to order of	NEGOTIABLE FIATA COMBINED TRANSPORT BILL OF LADING — ICC issued subject to ICC Uniform Rules for a Combined Transport Document (ICC publication 298)

Notify address

Place of Receipt	
Ocean Vessel	Port of Loading
Port of Discharge	Place of Delivery

Marks and Numbers	Number and Kind of Packages	Description of Goods	Gross Weight	Measurement

FOR INFORMATION

according to the declaration of the consignor.
The goods and instructions are accepted and dealt with subject to the Standard Conditions printed overleaf.

Taken in charge in apparent good order and condition, unless otherwise noted herein, at the place of receipt for transport and delivery as mentioned above.

One of these Combined Transport Bills of Lading must be surrendered duly endorsed in exchange for the goods. In Witness whereof the original Combined Transport Bills of Lading all of this tenor and date have been signed in the number stated below, one of which being accomplished the other(s) to be void.

Freight Amount	Freight Payable at	Place and date of Issue Stamp and signature
Cargo Insurance through the undersigned ☐ not covered ☐ Covered according to attached Policy	Number of Original FBL's	
For delivery of goods please apply to		

Text authorized by F.I.A.T.A. copyright FIATA/Zurich – Switzerland 5.84

(Reproduced by permission of The Institute of Freight Forwarders)

Appendix I

HOUSE BILL OF LADING

SHIPPED by or RECEIVED for shipment from in apparent good order and condition, except as noted in the Particulars.

Shipper	B/Lading Number	Customs Reference/Status
		Shipper's Reference
(hereinafter called the Shipper)		Forwarder's Reference
Consignee (If 'Order' State Notify Party and Address)		

Notify Party and Address (leave blank if stated above)

Place of Receipt

Conveyance | Point of Loading

Point of Discharge | Destination

HOUSE BILL OF LADING
Contents, weight, value and measurement according to sender's declaration

Marks, Nos and Container No. | Number and Kind of Packages; Description of Goods | Gross Weight (Kg) | Cube (M³)

REV 6.87

FOR INFORMATION

This house Bill of Lading shall have effect subject to the Standard Trading Conditions of the Institute of Freight Forwarders Ltd, as printed overleaf. Your attention is particularly drawn to: – Clauses 3 (B), 15, 23(A) and 33-35 inclusive.

Approved by SITPRO
Recommended by the Institute of Freight Forwarders

IN WITNESS whereof the Undersigned have signed the number of Bills of Lading shown all of this tenor and date. One Bill of Lading, duly endorsed, is to be given up in exchange for the goods or for a delivery order for same upon which the other Bills of Lading contained in the set shall be void.

Freight Payable at | Place and Date of Issue

Number of Original Bs/Lading | For and on behalf of

For particulars of delivery apply with this Bill of Lading to

(Reproduced by permission of the Institute of Freight Forwarders)

How to Export

AIR WAYBILL

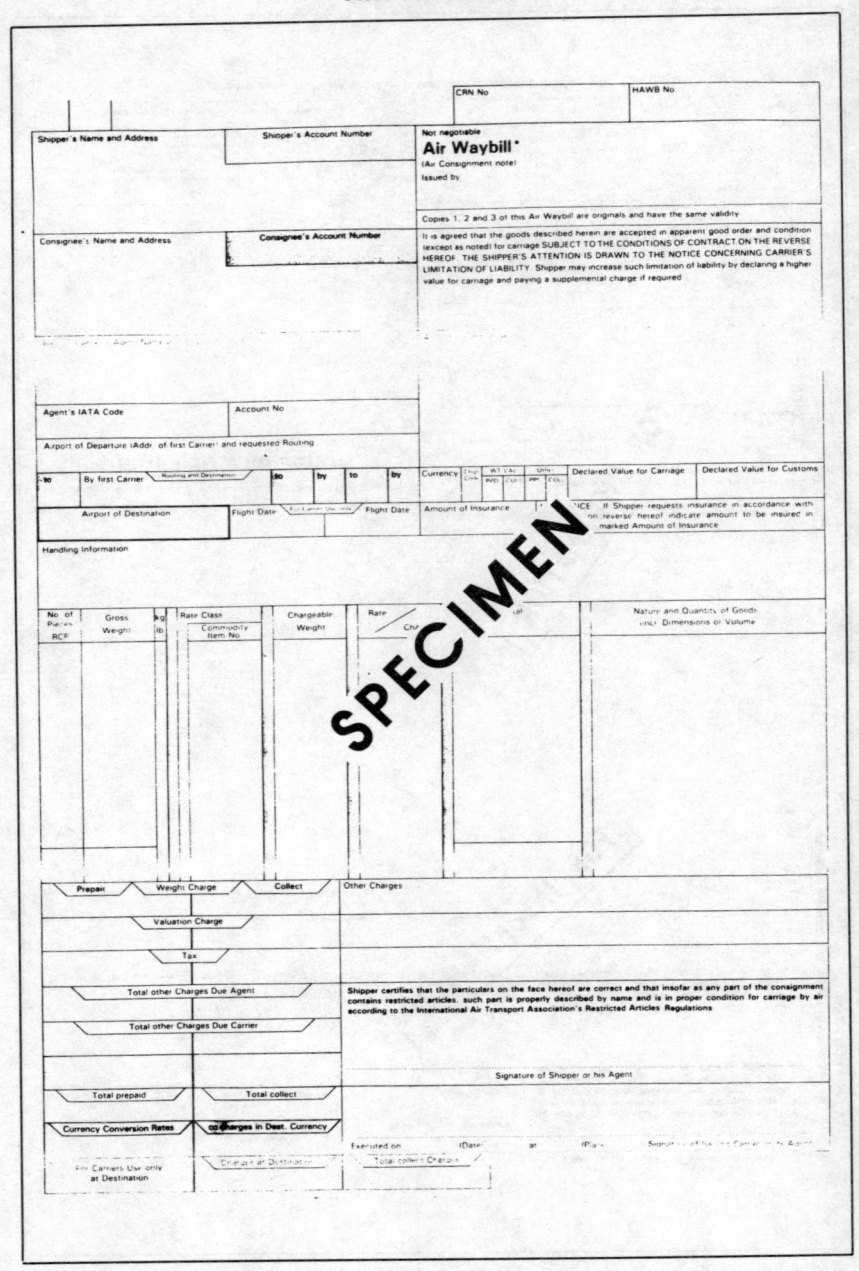

(Specimen form)

Appendix I

CMR NOTE

How to Export

CERTIFICATE OF INSURANCE

No.

SUN ALLIANCE INSURANCE GROUP
INCORPORATING PHOENIX ASSURANCE
Marine Division—U.K., Richmond House, 1 Rumford Place, Liverpool L3 9QU

Certificate of Marine Insurance

THIS IS TO CERTIFY that SUN ALLIANCE AND LONDON INSURANCE plc (hereinafter called the Company) has insured under Policy No. the undermentioned goods for the voyage and value stated on behalf of

CONDITIONS of INSURANCE

Institute Cargo Clauses (A) but sendings by Air (other than by Post) subject to the Institute Cargo Clauses (Air) (excluding sendings by Post)
Institute War Clauses
Institute Strikes Clauses } appropriate to the mode of transit to which this Certificate applies.
Institute Replacement Clause
Replacement Clause (Second-hand Machinery) } if applicable
Institute Classification Clause

(The Institute Clauses referred to are those current at time of commencement of risk)

Shipped (per Vessel, Aircraft, etc.)   From (Commencement of transit)

Via   To (final destination)   Insured Value and Currency

Marks and Numbers   Interest

SPECIMEN

SHIPPED UNDER DECK BUT CONTAINER SHIPMENTS ON OR UNDER DECK

SURVEYS
In the event of loss or damage for which the Company may be liable, immediate notice must be given to

in order that a Surveyor may, if necessary, be appointed

CLAIMS payable at   by

Signed on behalf of and under the authority of
Sun Alliance and London Insurance plc
BAIN CLARKSON LIMITED UK DIVISION

Date of issue

This Certificate may require to be stamped within a given period in order to conform with the laws of the country of destination. Holders are therefore advised to ascertain the amount of Stamp Duty, if any, required.

THIS CERTIFICATE REQUIRES ENDORSEMENT BY THE ASSURED.   **IMPORTANT — See Over**

(Reproduced by permission of Bain Clarkson Limited)

Appendix I

BILL OF EXCHANGE

N° 1234

Drawn under Credit Number 01/765/NWB/2A of Traders Bank of Japan, Tokyo, Japan, dated 1 November 1984

19th November 19 84 For £100,000

At SIGHT Pay this SOLE of Exchange to the Order

of OURSELVES

THE SUM OF ONE HUNDRED THOUSAND POUNDS STERLING

Value RECEIVED which place to Account

To NATIONAL WESTMINSTER BANK PLC
25, OLD BROAD STREET
LONDON EC12

UNITED KINGDOM SELLER LIMITED

C. Drr.

SPECIMEN

(Reproduced by permission of National Westminster Bank plc)

How to Export

LETTER OF CREDIT

National Westminster Bank PLC
International Banking Division
Documentary Credits Department – Overseas Branch

United Kingdom Seller Limited
Baltic House
27 Leadenhall Street
London EC3

Dear Sirs

We have been requested by Traders Bank of Japan, Tokyo, Japan to advise the issue of their irrevocable credit Number 01/765 in your favour for account of JAPAN BUYER CORPORATION c/o NYK Line 3-2 Marunouchi 2-Chome, Chiyoda-ku, Tokyo 100, Japan for £100,000 (SAY ONE HUNDRED THOUSAND POUNDS STERLING).

available by your drafts on us at.......... sight accompanied by the following documents namely:

1. Signed Invoices in triplicate certifying goods are in accordance with Contract No. 1234 dated 23 October 1984 between Ja... ...ver Corporation and United Kingdom Seller Limited.

2. Marine and War Risk Insurance Certificate co... ...risks" warehouse to warehouse, for 10% above the CIF value, evi... ...c claims are payable in Japan.

3. Complete set 3/3 Shipping Company's cl... ...rd" ocean Bills of Lading made out to order of the shippers an... ...co order of "Traders Bank of Japan", marked "Freight Paid" a... ...Japan Buyer Corporation c/o NYK Line 3-2 Marunouchi 2-Chome... ..., Tokyo 100, Japan".

Covering: Mechanical Spare Part... ..., Japan.

Shipped from UK Port to Toky...

Partshipment prohibited ...nshipment prohibited

Documents must be presented fo... payment within 15 days from the date of shipment.

We are requested to add our confirmation to this Credit and we hereby undertake to pay you the face amount of your drafts drawn within its terms provided such drafts bear the number and date of the Credit and that the Letter of Credit and all amendments thereto are attached.

The Credit is subject to Uniform Customs and Practice for Documentary Credits (1983 Revision), International Chamber of Commerce Publication No. 400

Drafts drawn under this   [X] Payment
Credit must be presented to us for [ ] Negotiation not later than 14 December 1984
                                        [ ] Acceptance
and marked "Drawn under Credit Number 01/765/NWB/2A of Traders Bank of Japan, Tokyo, Japan   Dated 1 November 1984

SPECIMEN

Note: On the grounds of security the above Credit, whilst accurate in content, is used for illustrative purposes only.

(Reproduced by permission of National Westminster Bank plc)

Appendix I

CERTIFICATE OF ORIGIN

1 Consignor	No. PQ 134725	ORIGINAL
2 Consignee	**EUROPEAN COMMUNITY**	
	CERTIFICATE OF ORIGIN	
	3 Country of Origin	
4 Transport details (Optional)	5 Remarks	
6 Item number; marks, numbers, number and kind of packages; description of goods		7 Quantity

SPECIMEN

8 THE UNDERSIGNED AUTHORITY CERTIFIES THAT THE GOODS DESCRIBED ABOVE ORIGINATE IN THE COUNTRY SHOWN IN BOX 3

BIRMINGHAM CHAMBER OF INDUSTRY & COMMERCE

Place and date of issue; name, signature and stamp of competent authority

Birmingham

.....................19.....

Birmingham Chamber of Industry & Commerce

DTI/XP/1302.

(Reproduced by permission of Birmingham Chamber of Commerce and Industry)

How to Export

POSTAL CUSTOMS DECLARATION

POSTAL DESPATCH NOTE

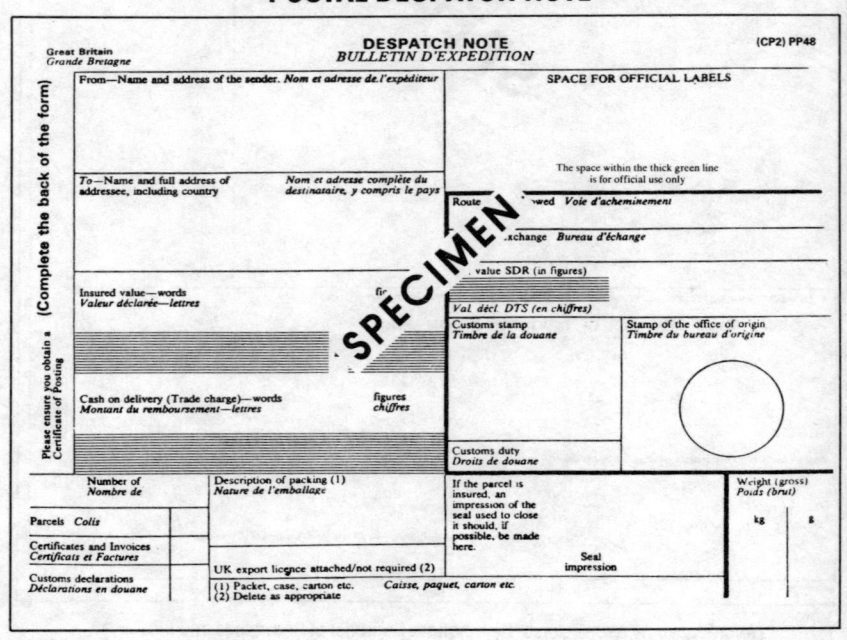

Appendix I

EUR1 MOVEMENT CERTIFICATE

1. Exporter (Name, full address, country)	**MOVEMENT CERTIFICATE** **EUR1 No.** P 410653 See notes overleaf before completing this form.
	2. Certificate used in preferential trade between
3. Consignee (Name, full address, country) (Optional)	**THE EUROPEAN ECONOMIC COMMUNITY** and .... (Insert appropriate countries or groups of countries or territories)
	4. Country, group of countries or territory in which the products are considered as originating **EEC**	5. Country, group of countries or territory of destination
6. Transport details (Optional)	7. Remarks

(1) If goods are not packed indicate number of articles or state "in bulk" as appropriate.

8. Item number: marks & numbers	Number and kind of packages (1): description of goods	9. Gross weight (kg) or other measure (litres, cu. m., etc.)	10. Invoices (Optional)

SPECIMEN

(2) Complete only where the regulations of the exporting country or territory require.

11. CUSTOMS ENDORSEMENT	12. DECLARATION BY THE EXPORTER
Declaration certified Stamp Export document (2): Form:_____ No._____ Customs office _____ Issuing country or territory: **UNITED KINGDOM** Date.. .... (Signature)	I, the undersigned, declare that the goods described above meet the conditions required for the issue of this certificate. (Place and date) .... (Signature)

C 1299   1   F 4990 (August, 1984)   Printed in the UK for HMSO
 Dd. 8858197 9/85 FCS 0694

(Crown Copyright. Reproduced by permission of HMSO)

How to Export

SINGLE ADMINISTRATIVE DOCUMENT C88 (1-8)

(All SAD Form(s) are Crown Copyright. Reproduced by permission of HMSO.)

Appendix I

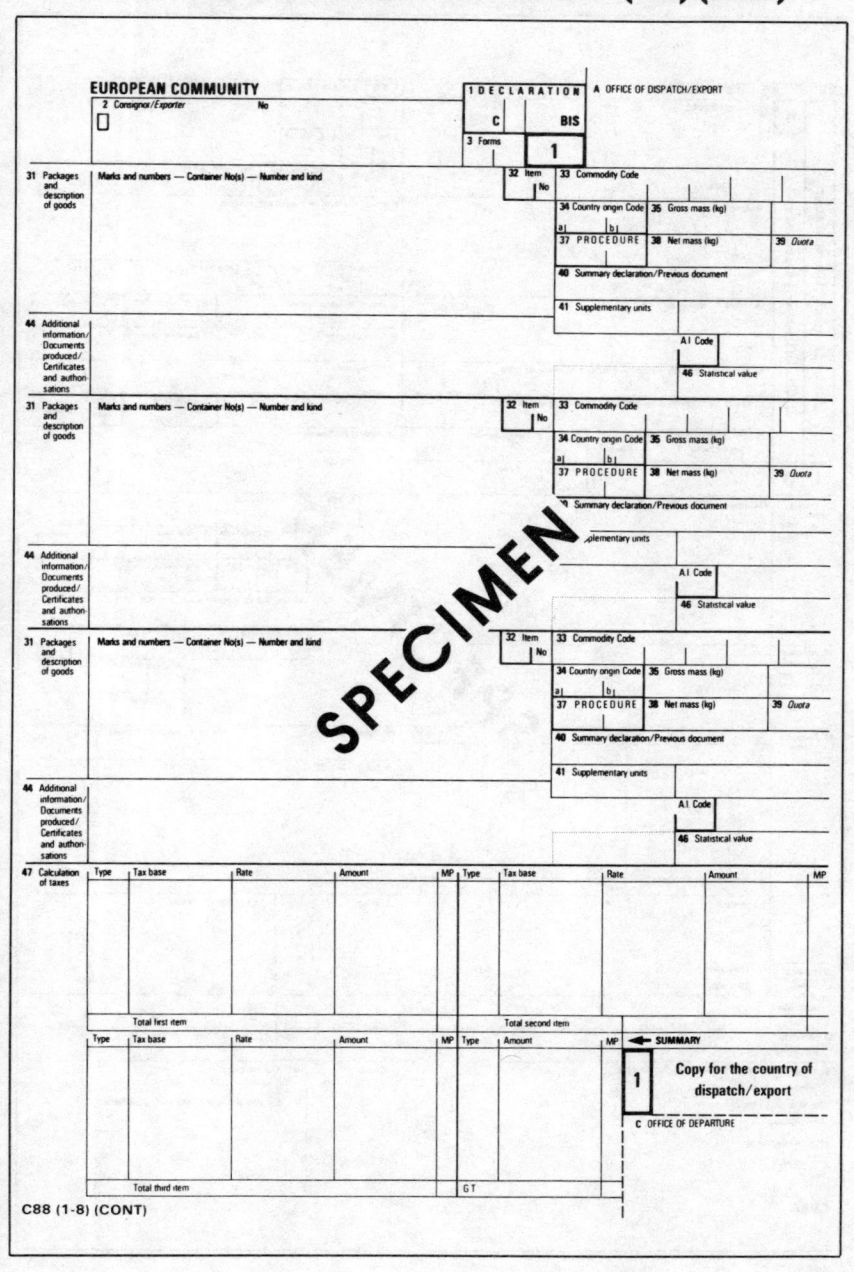

SINGLE ADMINISTRATIVE DOCUMENT C88 (1-8) (Cont.)

How to Export

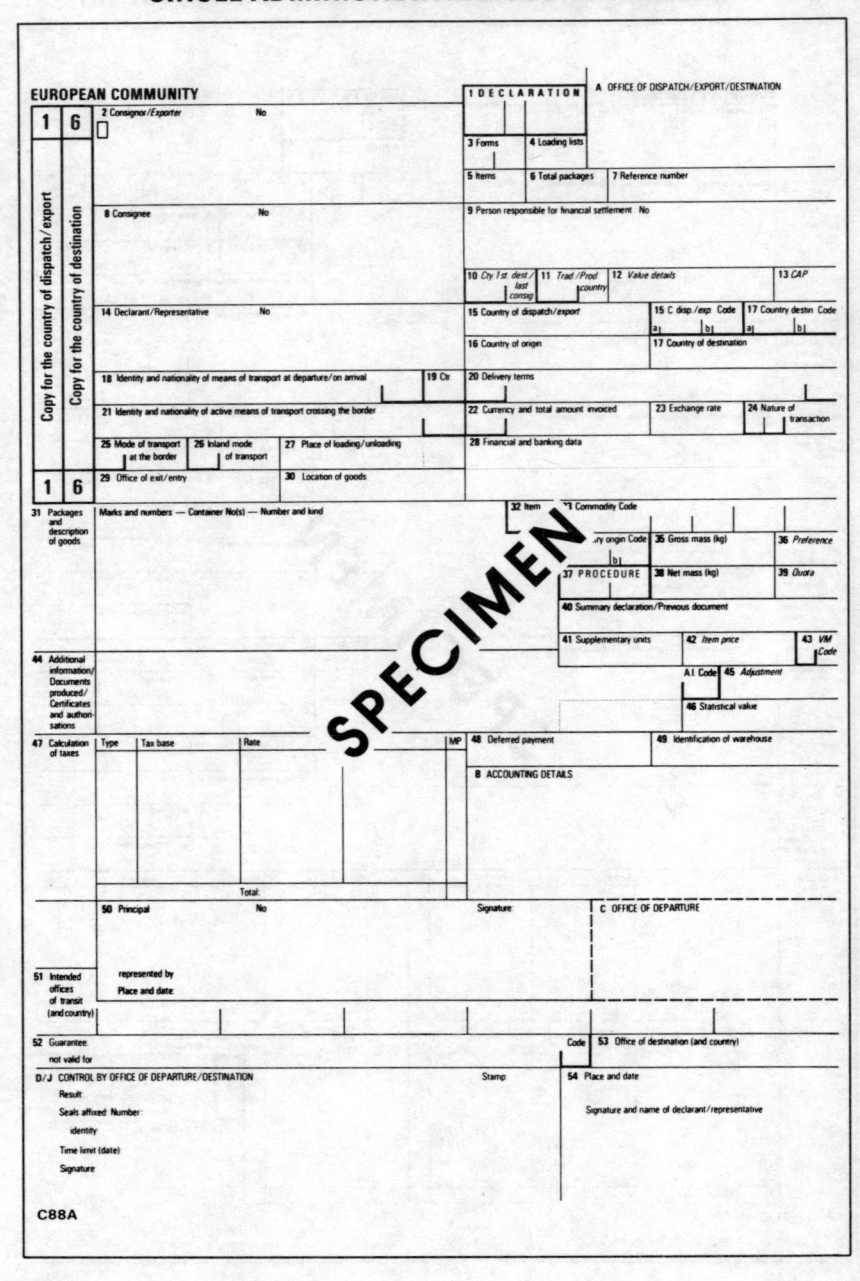

SINGLE ADMINISTRATIVE DOCUMENT C88A

Appendix I

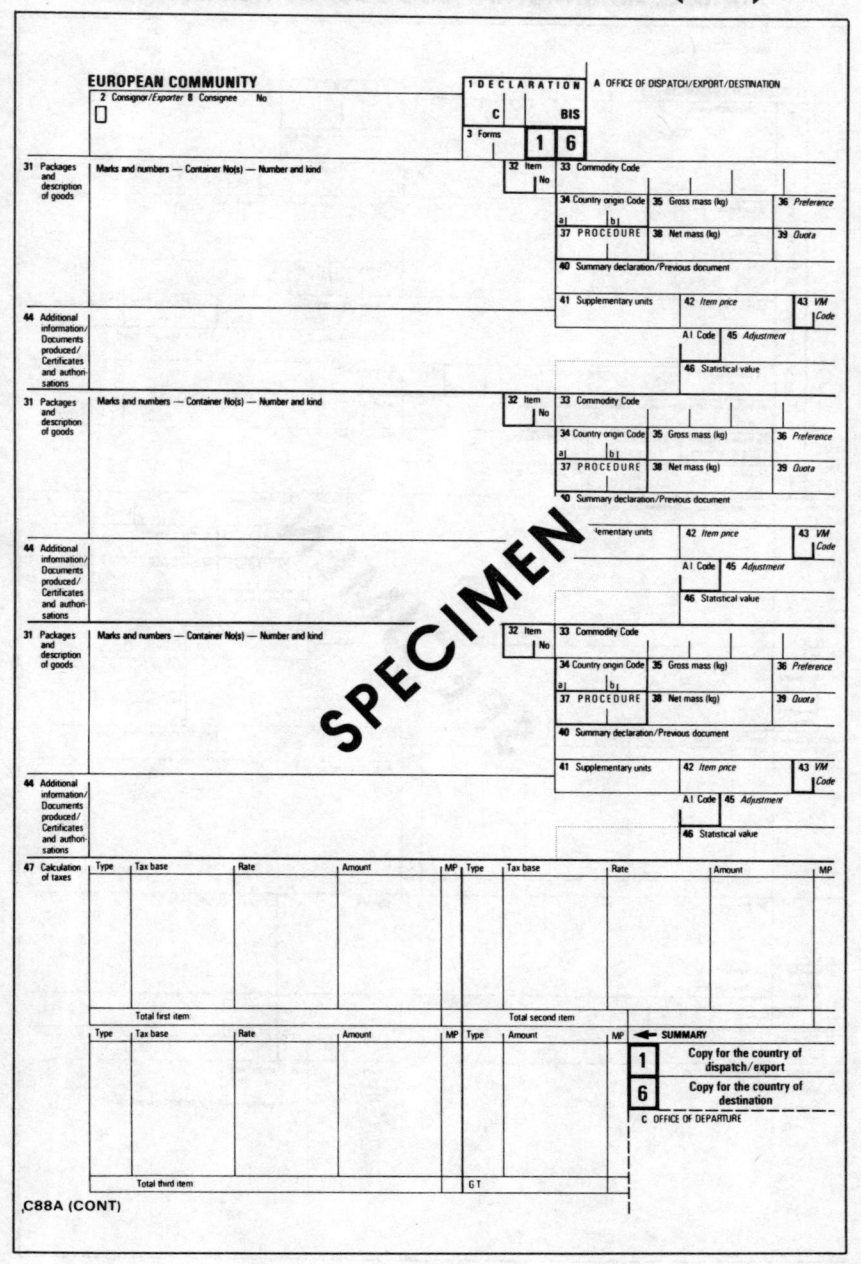

SINGLE ADMINISTRATIVE DOCUMENT C88A (Cont.)

How to Export

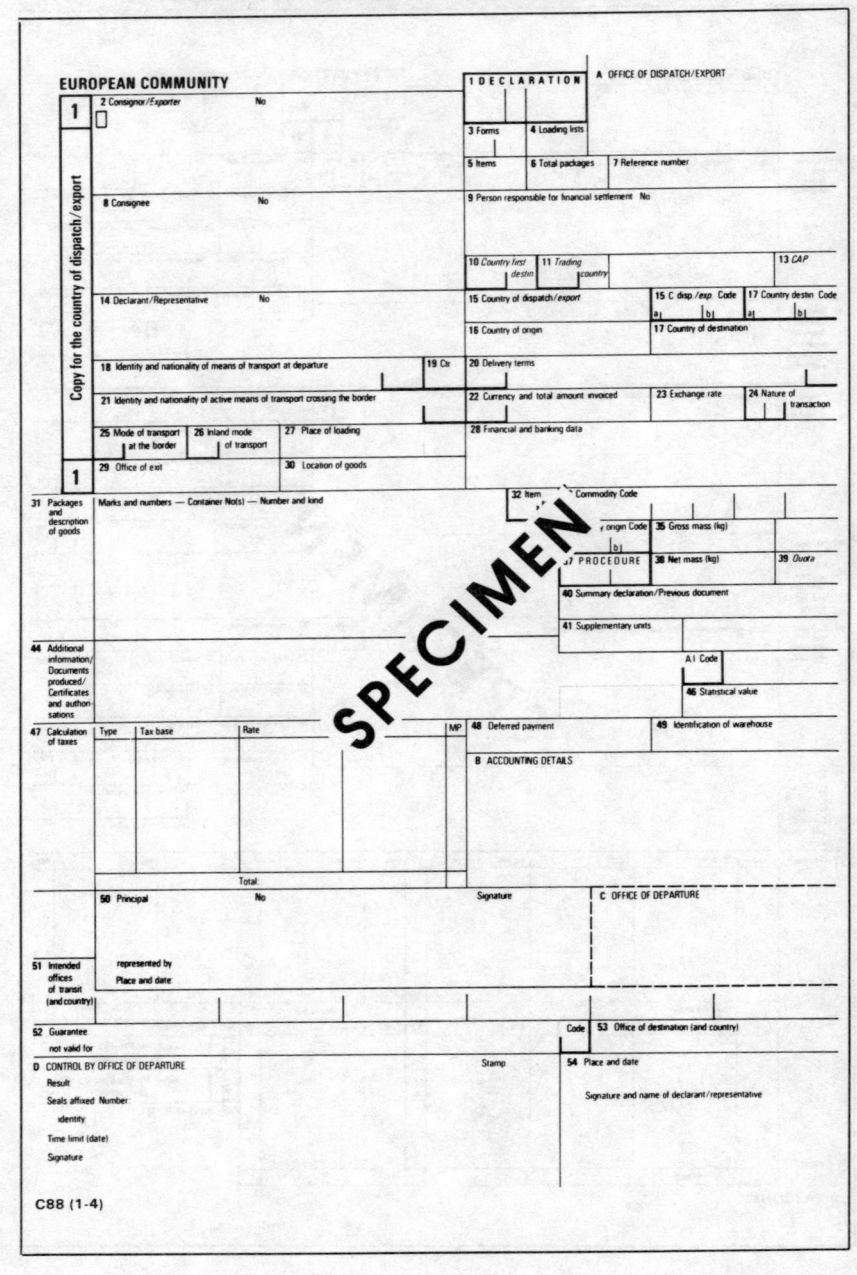

SINGLE ADMINISTRATIVE DOCUMENT C88 (1-4)

EUROPEAN COMMUNITY

1 — Copy for the country of dispatch/export

2 Consignor/Exporter No

1 DECLARATION **A OFFICE OF DISPATCH/EXPORT**

3 Forms | 4 Loading lists
5 Items | 6 Total packages | 7 Reference number

8 Consignee No

9 Person responsible for financial settlement No

10 Country first destn | 11 Trading country | 13 CAP

14 Declarant/Representative No

15 Country of dispatch/export | 15 C disp./exp. Code | 17 Country destn Code

16 Country of origin | 17 Country of destination

18 Identity and nationality of means of transport at departure | 19 Ctr | 20 Delivery terms

21 Identity and nationality of active means of transport crossing the border | 22 Currency and total amount invoiced | 23 Exchange rate | 24 Nature of transaction

25 Mode of transport at the border | 26 Inland mode of transport | 27 Place of loading | 28 Financial and banking data

29 Office of exit | 30 Location of goods

31 Packages and description of goods — Marks and numbers — Container No(s) — Number and kind

32 Item | Commodity Code
origin Code | 35 Gross mass (kg)
37 PROCEDURE | 38 Net mass (kg) | 39 Quota
40 Summary declaration/Previous document
41 Supplementary units

44 Additional information/Documents produced/Certificates and authorisations

A I Code
46 Statistical value

SPECIMEN

47 Calculation of taxes | Type | Tax base | Rate | MP | 48 Deferred payment | 49 Identification of warehouse

B ACCOUNTING DETAILS

Total

50 Principal No | Signature | **C OFFICE OF DEPARTURE**

51 Intended offices of transit (and country) | represented by | Place and date:

52 Guarantee not valid for | Code | 53 Office of destination (and country)

D CONTROL BY OFFICE OF DEPARTURE | Stamp | 54 Place and date
Result
Seals affixed Number: | Signature and name of declarant/representative
identity
Time limit (date)
Signature

C88 (1-4)

Appendix I

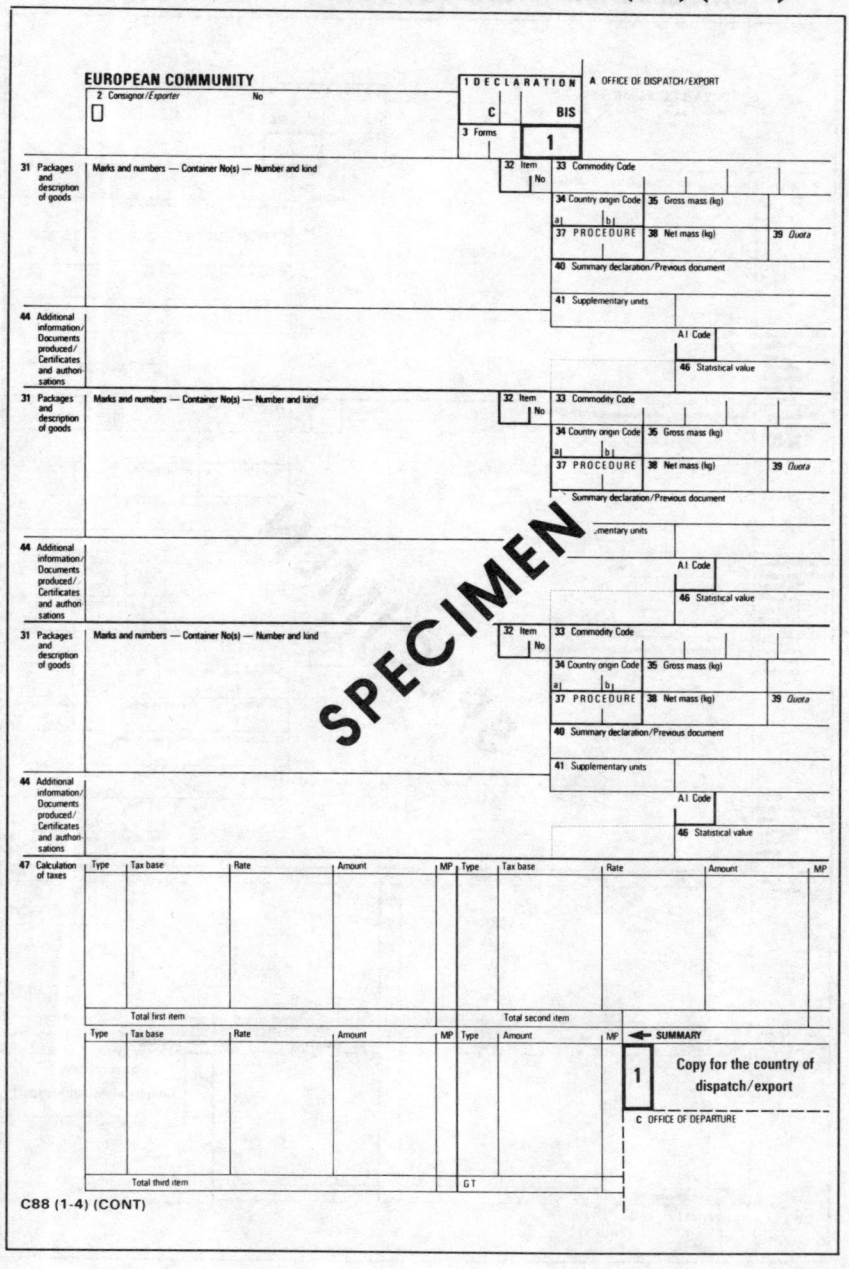

SINGLE ADMINISTRATIVE DOCUMENT C88 (1-4) (Cont.)

How to Export

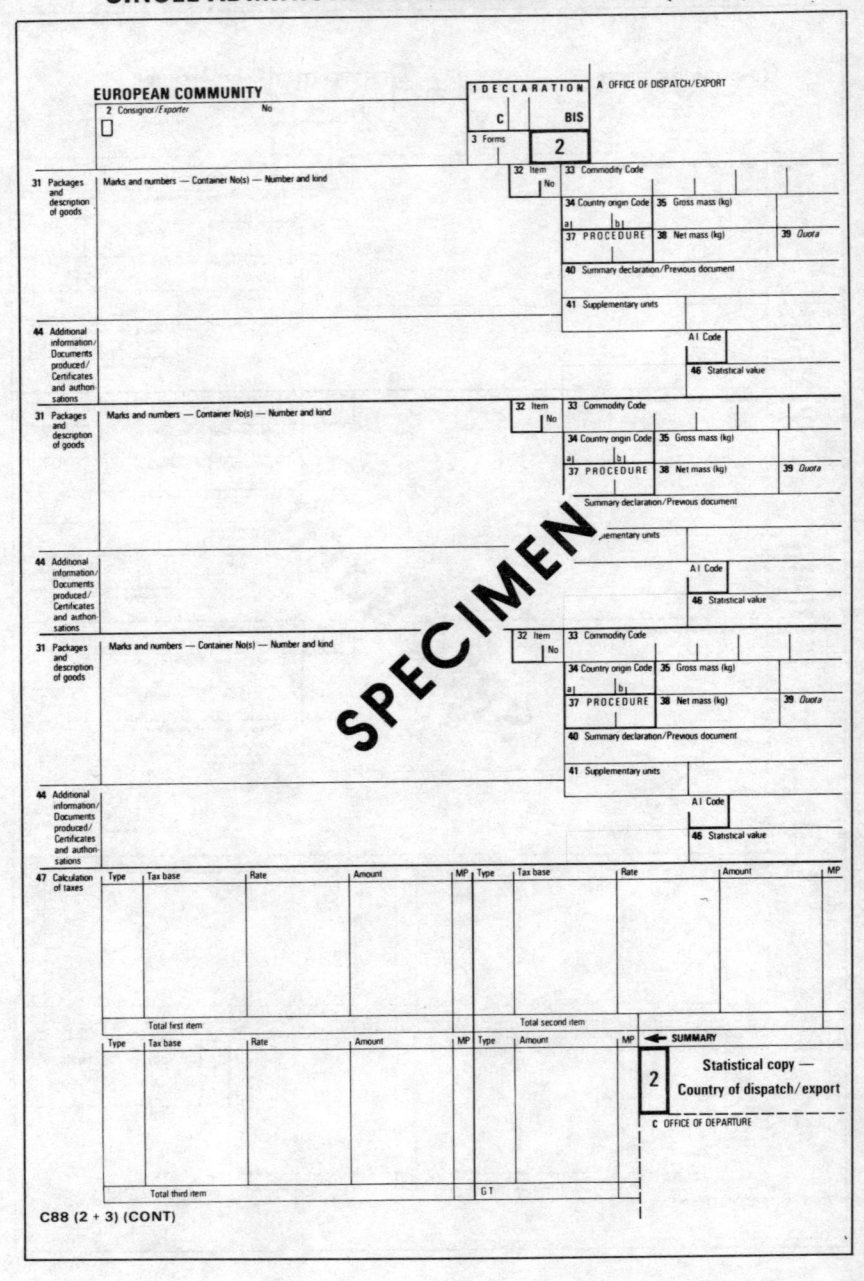

SINGLE ADMINISTRATIVE DOCUMENT C88 (2 & 3)

SPECIMEN form — Statistical copy — Country of dispatch/export

Appendix I

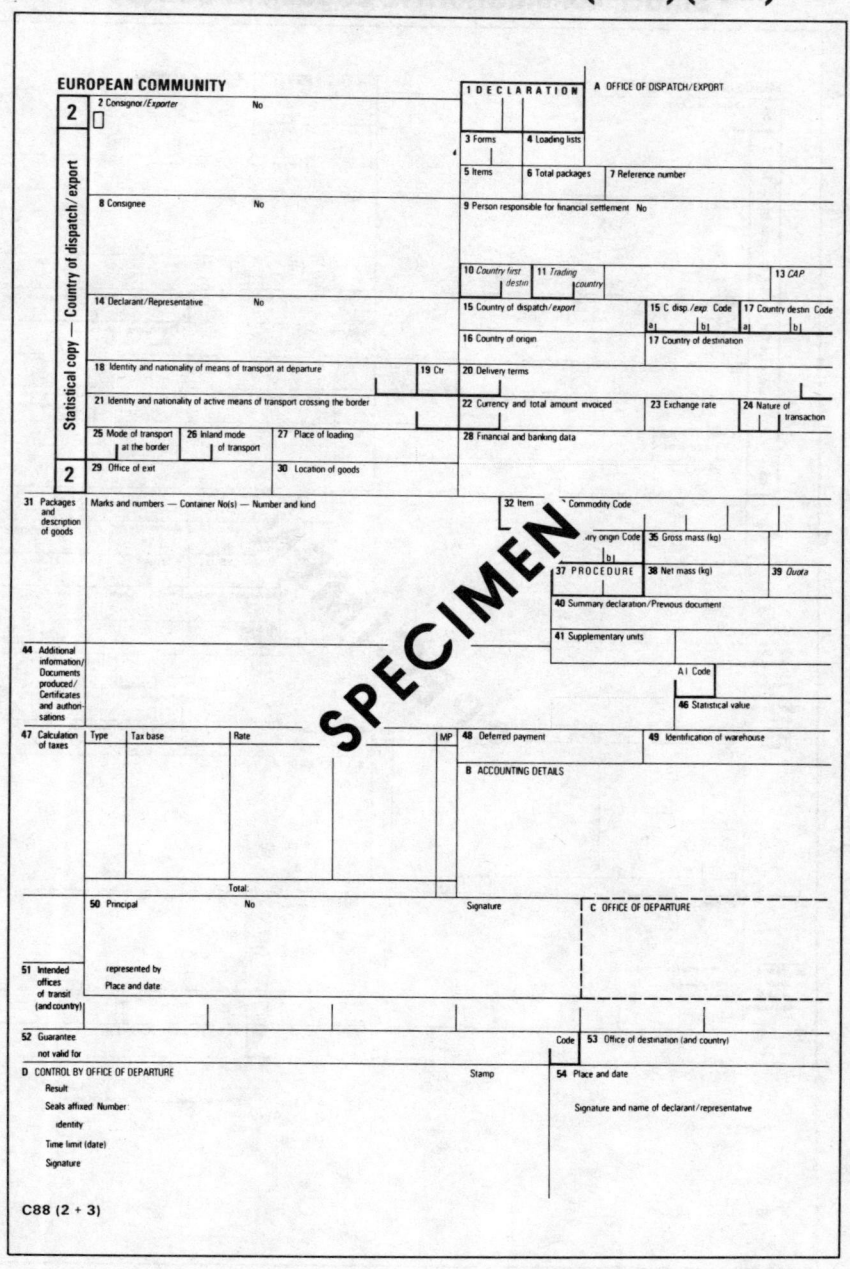

SINGLE ADMINISTRATIVE DOCUMENT C88 (2 & 3) (Cont.)

How to Export

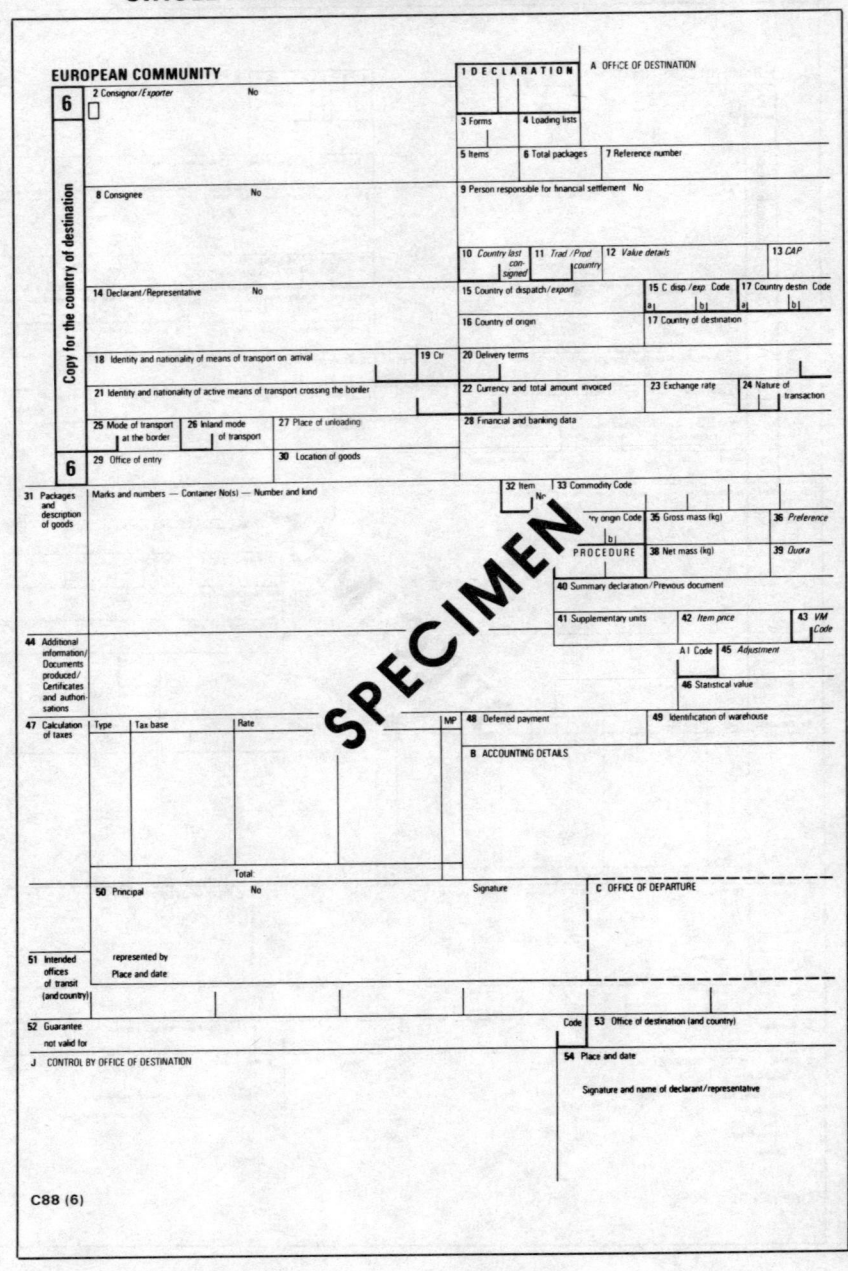

SINGLE ADMINISTRATIVE DOCUMENT C88 (6)

Appendix I

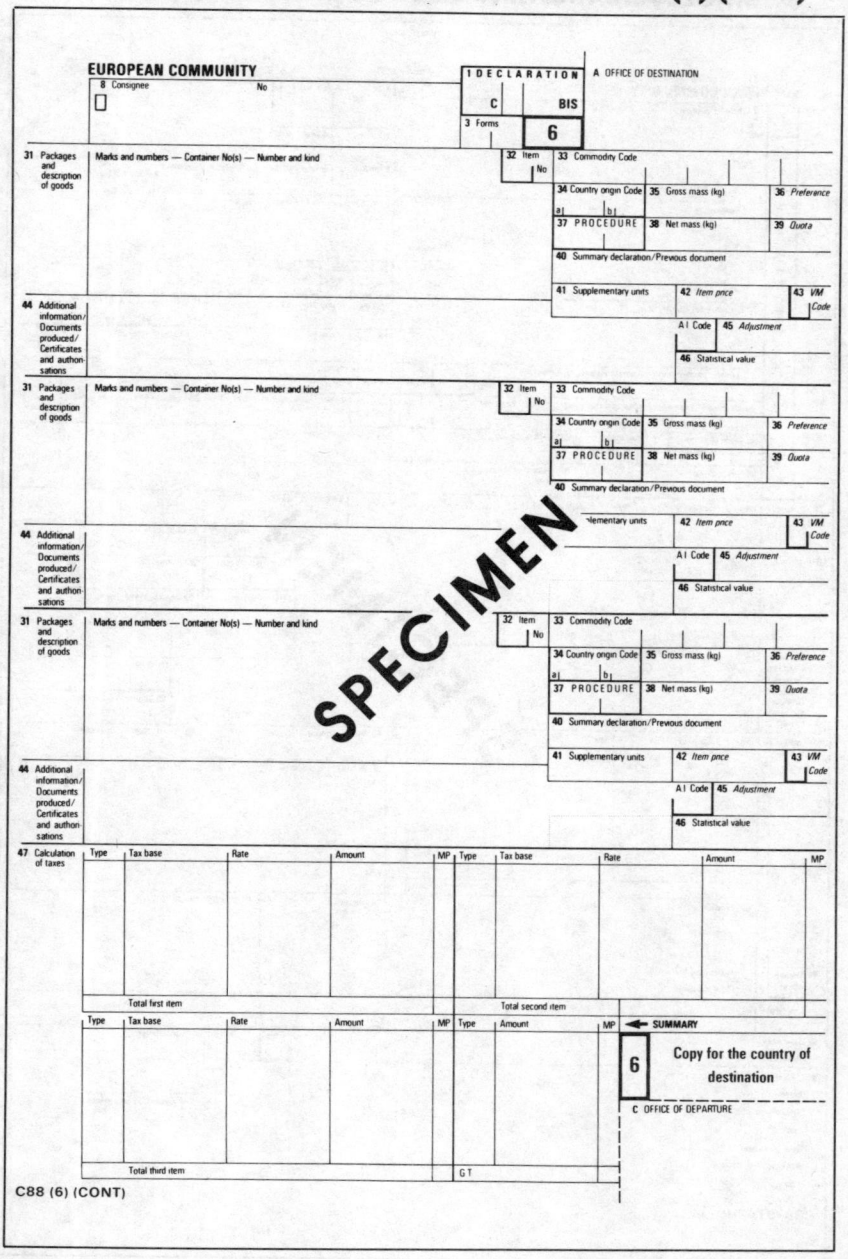

SINGLE ADMINISTRATIVE DOCUMENT C88 (6) (Cont.)

How to Export

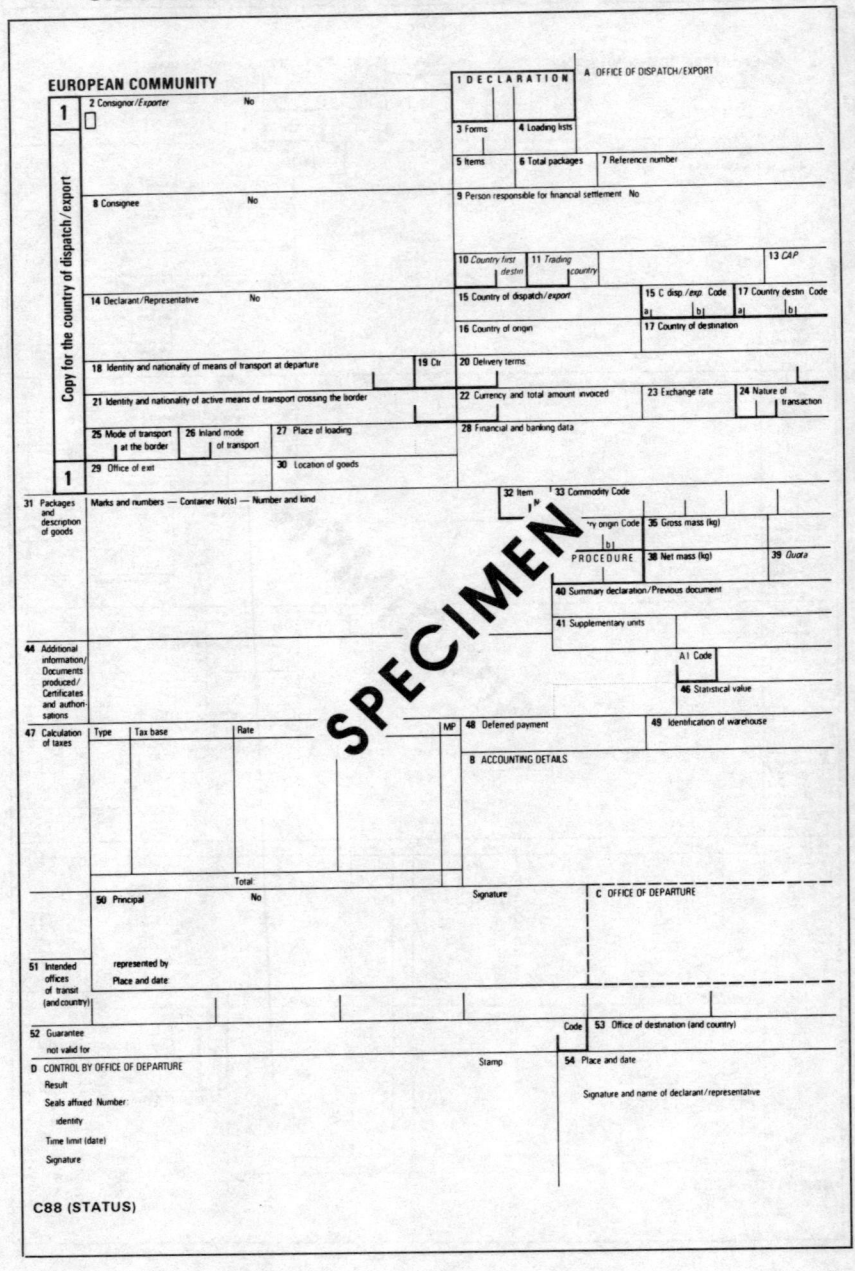

SINGLE ADMINISTRATIVE DOCUMENT C88 (STATUS)

Appendix I

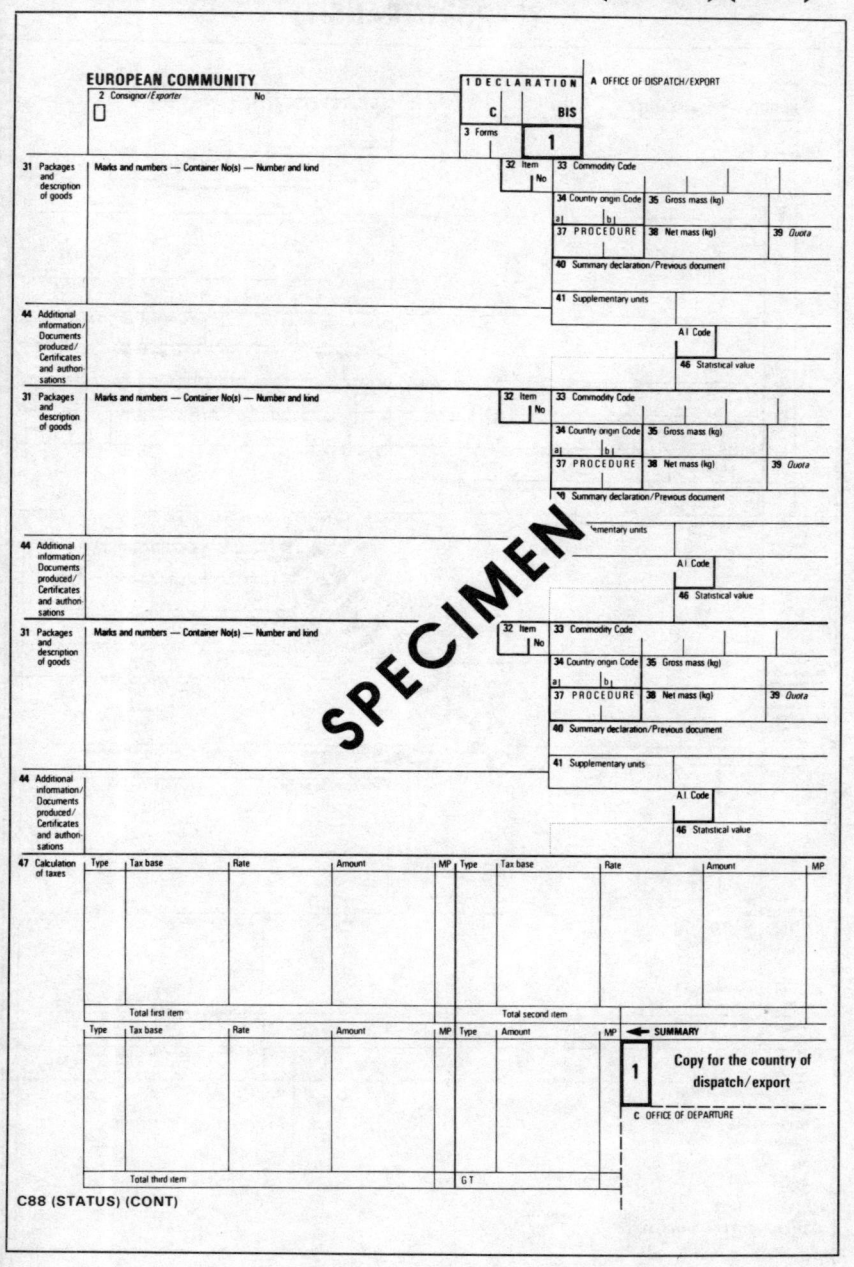

SINGLE ADMINISTRATIVE DOCUMENT C88 (STATUS) (Cont.)

How to Export

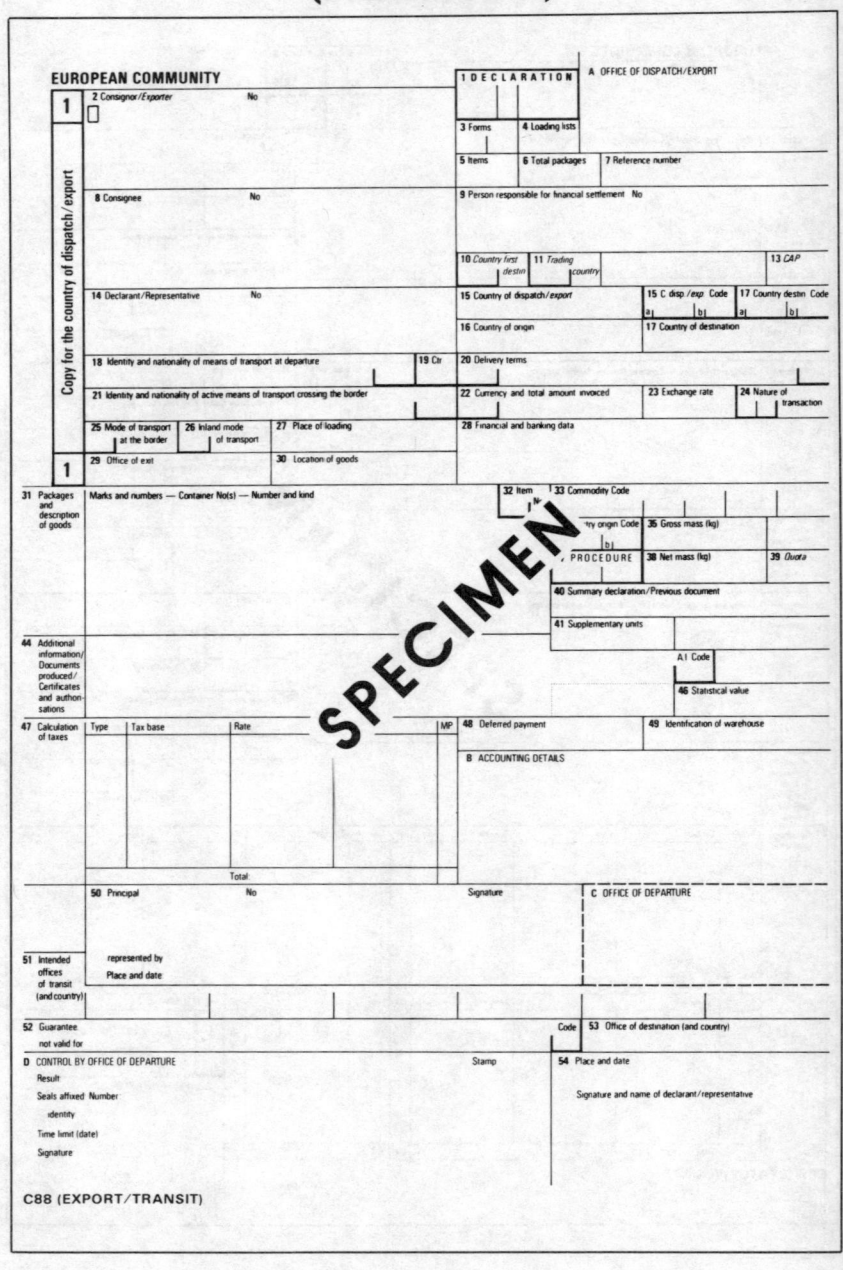

SINGLE ADMINISTRATIVE DOCUMENT C88
(EXPORT/TRANSIT)

[SPECIMEN form — European Community Single Administrative Document C88 (Export/Transit), Copy for the country of dispatch/export, containing numbered fields 1–54 and lettered sections A–D]

Appendix I

SINGLE ADMINISTRATIVE DOCUMENT C88
(EXPORT/TRANSIT) (Cont.)

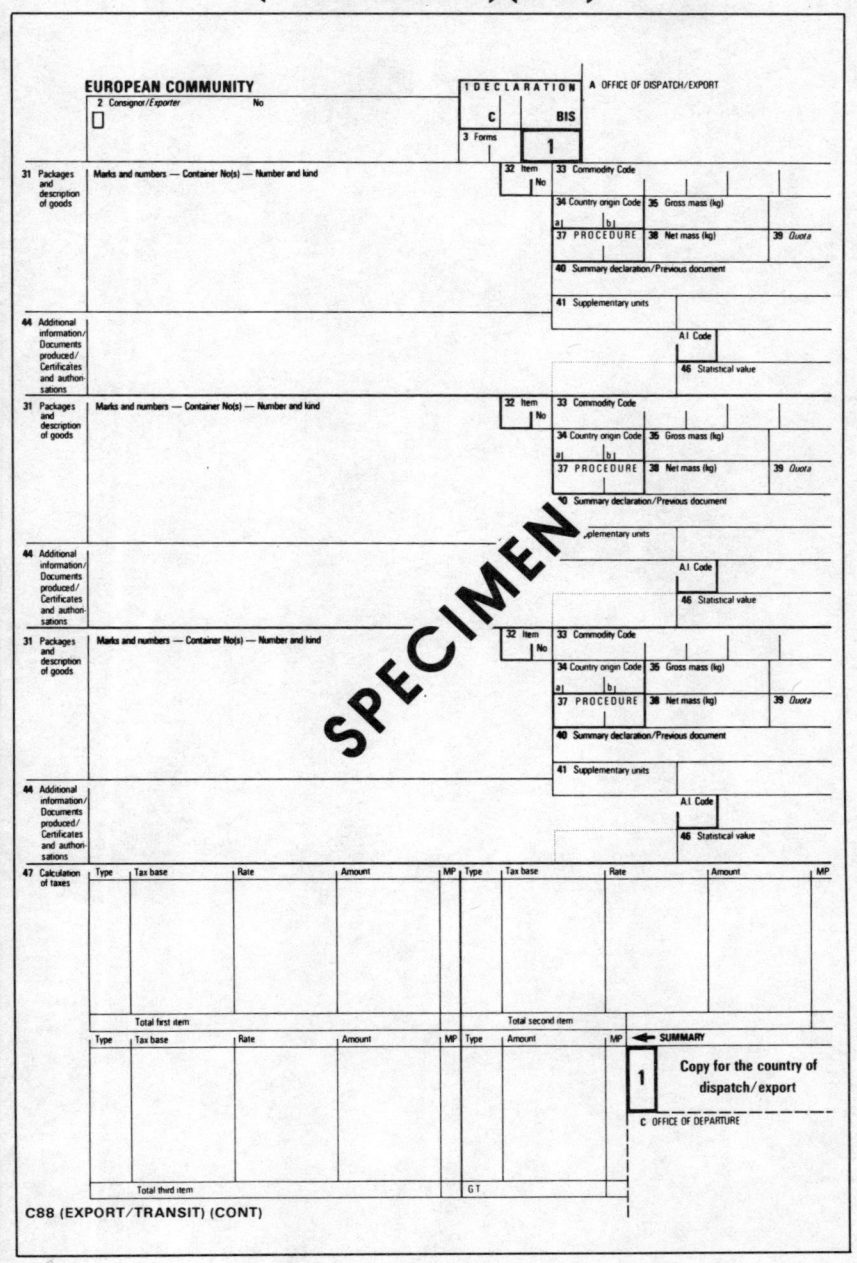

Appendix II

Exporter's checklist

Setting Up
☐ Decide whether to use an export administration company and if so which of these points they will cover.
☐ Find a good freight forwarder.
☐ Talk to your postal services representative.
☐ Talk to your Chamber of Commerce.
☐ Talk to an international specialist from your bank.
☐ Check if you can take further advantage of other export services, such as those of the British Overseas Trade Board (BOTB).

At the Market Research Stage
☐ Check competitors' delivery terms (ex-works to delivered).
☐ Check competitors' currency of sale (probably buyer's currency).
☐ Check competitors' terms of payment (30, 60, 180 days, Letter of Credit, and so on).
☐ Check normal methods of transport and obtain quotations.
☐ Check if subject to special controls or financial arrangements, such as for processed foodstuffs, or textiles.

At the Quotation Stage
☐ Consult your freight forwarder and bank as necessary.
☐ Quote delivery terms and include these costs in the price.
☐ Quote in suitable currency.
☐ Specify a suitable method of transport.
☐ Quote the terms and methods of payment clearly.

How to Export

When the order is received
- ☐ Check that the terms are as quoted and all delivery, paperwork, and payment requirements can be met.
- ☐ Arrange cover against foreign currency fluctuations and default.

When the order is ready – or preferably beforehand
- ☐ Contact the forwarder to arrange transport and insurance.
- ☐ Allow time to complete and process the documents, especially the special certificates or methods of payment where other organisations are involved.

At regular intervals until payment is in your bank account
- ☐ Check progress of payment and other commercial factors, such as the customer's total indebtedness to you.
- ☐ Check cumulative costs of interest, both from date of invoice and back to the date of receipt of order.

When payment has been received
- ☐ Check whether the intended margin has been realised after deducting all costs and overheads.
- ☐ Review the success of the transaction and what points to improve on next time.

COSTPOINTS – FEES, CHARGES AND OTHER COSTS
- ☐ Carriage to point of delivery.
- ☐ Insurance to point of delivery.
- ☐ Fees for forwarder's export services.
- ☐ Fees for import services (if selling delivered).
- ☐ Cost of covering against exchange-rate fluctuations.
- ☐ Fees for special documents, eg stamping Certificates of Origin.
- ☐ Refunds or levies for certain processed foods.
- ☐ Interest charges on credit sales, or discounts/ fees on bank's up-front settlements.
- ☐ Bank fees for services debited to you.
- ☐ Insurance against default by customer.
- ☐ Communications costs – airmail, telex, telephone.
- ☐ Time cost at up to £10 per day for each £1,000 per annum salary.

(Reproduced by permission of SITPRO)

Appendix III

Glossary of commonly used export conditions of sale

Cost and Freight (C&F)
As per CIF except that the buyer is responsible for all insurance charges.

Cost, Insurance and Freight (CIF)
All the costs of freight and insurance to the port or airport specified by the customer are met by the supplier. Delivery takes place and title passes once the Bill of Landing is tendered to the buyer.

Ex-Ship
All transport and insurance charges, including inward port dues, are the responsibility of the supplier. Goods, and commensurate risks, pass to the buyer when the vessel on which they were shipped is able and willing to discharge the goods.

Ex Works (EXW)
The Customer arranges for the goods to be collected from the supplier's premises. He is also responsible for all freight and insurance costs. Once the customer has been notified that the goods are ready for collection all risks pass to him.

Franco Warehouse or Franco Domicile (DDP)
The supplier bears responsibility for all charges to a warehouse at an agreed destination, or to the buyer's own warehouse. Responsibility for the goods and the risks attached

to them passes to the buyer once the goods reach the agreed warehouse or the buyer's own premises. This may, or may not, include customs duty and clearance charges. For example, where it is included documents should read 'Franco Warehouse duty paid'.

Free Alongside Ship (FAS)
The supplier is responsible for the goods and all costs until the consignment reaches the port of despatch and is safely alongside the appropriate vessel. 'Alongside' is normally defined as being under the ship's loading hooks. Goods and risk pass to the buyer when the vessel is ready and able to load its cargo.

Free on Board (FOB)
The supplier is responsible for placing the goods onboard the ship or aircraft as designated by the customer. He is also responsible for all charges up to that point. The customer arranges and pays for freight and insurance. The goods pass to him, as do the risks, once they have been loaded onboard, unless otherwise specified in the original contract.

Free on Rail (FOR)
The same principles apply as for FOB except that the goods are to be transported by rail.

Free on Truck (FOT)
Here again, the supplier's responsibility for the goods and the risk attached thereto, ceases once the goods have been loaded onto the road transport stipulated by the customer.

Landed or Franco Quay (EXQ)
All charges, including unloading from vessel and any quay charges at the destination port, are met by the supplier. Goods and risks pass to the buyer once the goods have landed.

Appendix IV

List of useful names and addresses

Association of British
Travel Agents (ABTA)
55-57 Newman St
London W1P 4AH
01-637 2444

Association of British
Chambers of Commerce
Sovereign House
212a Shaftesbury Avenue
London WC2H 8EW
01-240 5831

Automobile Association
(AA)
Fanum House
Basingstoke
Hants RG21 2EA
0256 20123

British Overseas Trade
Board (BOTB)
1 Victoria St
London SW1H 0EY
01-215 7877

Regional Offices as follows:

East Midlands
Severn House
20 Middle Pavement
Nottingham NG1 7DW
0602 506181
Telex: 37143

North East
Stanegate House
2 Groat Market
Newcastle upon Tyne
NE1 1YN
091 232 4722

Northern Ireland
Industrial Development
Board for
Northern Ireland
IDB House
64 Chichester St
Belfast BT1 4JX
0232 233233
Telex: 747025

How to Export

North West
Sunley Building
Piccadilly Plaza
Manchester M1 4BA
061 236 2171
Telex: 667104

Scotland
Industry Dept for Scotland
Alhambra House
45 Waterloo St
Glasgow G2 6AT
041 248 2855
Telex: 777883

South East
Ebury Bridge House
Ebury Bridge Road
London SW1W 8QD
01-730 9678
Telex: 297124/5/6

South West
The Pithay
Bristol BS1 2PB
0272 272666
Telex: 44214

Wales
New Crown Building
Cathays Park
Cardiff CF1 3NQ
0222 825111
Telex: 498228

West Midlands
Ladywood House
Stephenson St
Birmingham B2 4DT
021 632 4111
Telex: 337919

Yorkshire and Humberside
Priestley House
1 Park Row
Leeds LS1 5LF
0532 443171
Telex: 557925

British Standards
Institution
No 2 Park St
London W1A 2BS
01-629 9000

Chambers of Commerce
(Refer to telephone
directory for your local
Chamber)

Croner Publications
Croner House
173 Kingston Road
New Malden
Surrey KT3 3SS
01-942 8966

Crown Agents
4 Millbank
London SW1P 3JD
01 222 7730

Dun and Bradstreet
26-32 Clifton St
London EC2P 2LY
01 377 4377
Telex: 886697

European Economic
Community (EEC)
8 Storey's Gate
London SW1P 3AT
01 222 8122

Appendix IV

Export Credits
Guarantee Dept
Aldermanbury House
Aldermanbury
London EC2P EL
01 382 7000
Telex: 883601

Croydon
Sunley House
Bedford Park
Croydon
Surrey CR9 4HL
01 680 5030
Telex: 946998

Regional offices as follows:

Belfast
12th Floor
Windsor House
9-15 Bedford St
Belfast BT2 7EG
0232 231743
Telex: 74577

Birmingham
Colmore Centre
115 Colmore Row
Birmingham B3 3SB
021 233 1771
Telex: 337332

Bristol
1 Redcliffe St
Bristol BS1 6NP
0272 299971
Telex: 44248

Cambridge
Three Crowns House
72-80 Hills Road
Cambridge CB2 1NJ
0223 68801
Telex: 81624

Glasgow
Fleming House
134 Renfrew St
Glasgow G3 6TL
041 332 8707
Telex: 77130

Leeds
West Riding House
67 Albion St
Leeds LS1 5AA
0532 450631
Telex: 55125

London
Export House
50 Ludgate Hill
London EC4M 7AY
01 726 4050
Telex: 8953044

Manchester
6th Floor
Townbury House
Blackfriars St
Salford M3 5AL
061 834 8181
Telex: 667756

How to Export

Exports Intelligence Service
Department of Trade
and Industry
Lime Grove
Eastcote
Ruislip
Middx HA4 8SG
01 866 8771 (Ext 266)
Telex: 888013

Export Network Ltd
31-37 Cursitor St
London
EC4A 1LT
01 430 0208

Exports to Europe Branch
Department of Trade
and Industry
1 Victoria St
London SW1H 0ET
01 215 4284
Telex: 27366/ 8811074

HM Customs and Excise
Kings Beam House
Mark Lane
London EC3R 7HE
01 626 1515
(Refer to telephone directory
for local offices)

Institute of Export
Export House
64 Clifton St
London EC2A 4HB
01 247 9812

Institute of Freight Forwarders
Suffield House
9 Paradise Road
Richmond
Surrey TW9 1SA
01 948 3141
Telex: 8953060

International Chambers of
Commerce UK
Centre Point
103 New Oxford St
London WC1A 1QB
01 240 5558

Overseas Chambers of
Commerce in London
American
75 Brook St
London W1Y 2EB
01 493 0381

Arab-British
26A Albemarle St
London W1A 4BL
01 499 3400

*Australian-British Trade
Association*
6th Floor
Dorland House
18-20 Lower Regent St
London SW1Y 4PW
01 930 2524
Telex: 8954430

*Austrian Commercial
Delegate in GB*
1 Hyde Park Gate
London SW7 5ER
01 584 6218
Telex: 25668

132

Appendix IV

Belgo-Luxembourg
36-37 Piccadilly
London W1V 0PL
01 434 1815
Telex: 8953411

Brazilian
35 Dover St
London W1X 3RA
01 499 0186

British-Soviet
2 Lowndes St
London SW1X 9ET
01 235 2423

Canada-UK
3 Lower Regent St
London SW1Y 4NZ
01 930 2794

French
54 Conduit St
London W1R 9SD
01 439 1735
Telex: 269132

German
12-13 Suffolk St
London SW1Y 4HG
01 930 7251

Hong Kong Trade Development Council
8 St James's Square
London SW1Y 4JZ
01 930 7955
Telex: 916923

Italian
Walmar House
296 Regent St
London W1R 6AE
01 637 3153
Telex: 269096

Netherlands-British
Dutch House
307-8 High Holborn
London WC1V 7LS
01 242 1064

New Zealand
Dorland House
18-20 Lower Regent St
London SW1Y 4PW
01 930 2524

Norwegian
Norway House
21-24 Cockspur St
London SW1Y 5BN
01 930 0181

Portuguese
New Bond Street House
1-5 New Bond St
London W1Y 9PE
01 493 9973

Spanish
5 Cavendish Square
London W1M 0DP
01 637 9061
Telex: 8811583

Swedish Trade Commission
73 Welbeck St
London W1M 8AN
01 935 9601
Telex: 22620

Yugoslav Economic Chamber
Crown House
143-7 Regent St
London W1R 7LB
01 734 2581
Telex: 27552

Paper and Board Printing &
Packaging Industry Research
Association
Randalls Road
Leatherhead
Surrey KT22 7RU
0372 376161

Road Haulage Association
104 New Kings Road
Fulham
London SW6 4LN
01 736 1183

Royal Automobile Club
(RAC)
PO Box 100
RAC House
Lansdowne Road
Croydon CR9 2JA
01 686 2525

Simplification of International
Trade Procedures Board
(SITPRO)
Almack House
26-28 King St
London SW1Y 6QW
01 930 0532
Telex: 919130
Fax: 01 930 5779

Statistics and Market Intelligence
Library
c/o BOTB
1 Victoria St
London SW1H 0EY
01 215 7877

Swedish Freight Forwarders
Association
(Sveriges Steditorfhorbund)
Ansgariegatan 10
S-11726 Stockholm
Sweden
010 46 8 08 84 4810

Appendix V
Seaports in the UK
Seaports
England and Wales

Althorpe	Dartmouth
Amble	Dover
Appledore	Ellesmere Port
Avonmouth	Exeter
Baltic Wharf, Rochford	Exmouth
Barrow-in-Furness	Falmouth
Barrow-on-Humber	Faversham
Barry Dock	Felixstowe
Barton-on-Humber	Fingringhoe
Beckingham	Fishguard
Berwick	Fleetwood
Bideford	Flixborough Wharf
Birkenhead	Folkestone
Blyth	Fowey
Boston	Gainsborough
Bridgwater	Garston
Bridlington	Glasson Dock
Bridport	Gloucester
Brightlingsea	Goole
Briton Ferry	Great Yarmouth
Brixham	Grimsby
Burnham-on-Crouch	Grove Wharves
Burton Stather	Guiness Wharf
Caernarfon	Hartlepool
Cardiff	Harwich
Charlestown	Heysham
Chepstow	Holehaven
Colchester	Holyhead
Cowes	Howdendyke

Hull	Portishead
Immingham	Portland
Ipswich	Portsmouth
Keadby	Port Talbot
Kings Lynn	Queenborough
Lancaster	Ramsgate
Leigh-on-Sea	Rhyl
Littlehampton	Ridham Dock
Liverpool	Rochester
Llanddulas	Rochford
Llanelli	Rowhedge
London	Royal Portbury Dock
Lowestoft	Runcorn
Lymington	Rye
Maldon	Scarborough
Manchester	Seaham
Medway	Selby
Middlesbrough	Sharpness
Milford	Sheerness
Millom	Shoreham
Mistley	Shotton
Moystyn	Silloth
Neap House	Southampton
Neath Abbey	Southend (Corporation Jetty)
Newcastle	South Shields
Newhaven	Sunderland
New Holland	Swansea
Newlyn	Teesport
Newport, Gwent	Teignmouth
North Shields	Tilbury
Northwich	Topsham
Norwich	Torquay
Padstow	Trent
Par	Truro
Parkeston Quay	Tyne
Partington	Warrington
Pembroke Ferry	Watchet
Pembroke (Oils) SO	Wells
Penryn	Weymouth
Penzance	Whitby
Plymouth	Whitehaven
Poole	Whitstable
Port Penrhyn	Wisbech

Appendix V

Wivenhoe
Workington
Isle of Man
Castletown
Douglas
Peel
Ramsey
Channel Islands
St Helier
St Peter Port
Scotland
Aberdeen
Annan
Arbroath
Ardrossan
Ayr
Barcaldine
Bowling
Buckie
Burghead
Burntisland
Campbeltown
Corpach, incl Annat Pier
Dundee
Faslane
Finnart
Fraserburgh
Furnace
Garlieston
Girvan
Glasgow
Grangemouth
Granton
Greenock
Hound Point Terminal

Hunterston
Invergordon
Inverness
Irvine
Islay
Kirkcaldy
Kirkwall
Leith
Lerwick
Lochaline
Lossiemouth
Macduff
Methil
Montrose
Oban
Palnackie
Perth
Peterhead
Scalloway
Scrabster
Stornoway
Stranraer
Stromness
Tayport
Ullapool
Wick
Northern Ireland
Belfast
Coleraine
Larne
Londonderry
Portrush
Warrenpoint
Land Boundary

Appendix VI

Inland clearance depots, inland rail depots and free zones

Inland clearance depots and inland rail depots

Barking Containerbase, Box Lane, Barking
Barking Containerway, International Freight Terminal, Ripple Road, Barking, Essex
Birmingham Containerbase, Perry Bar, Birmingham
Birmingham Inland Rail Depot, Landor Street, Birmingham
Bristol Inland Clearance Depot, Avonmouth
Coatbridge Containerbase, Coatbridge, Glasgow
Dagenham Storage Co. Ltd., Dagenham, Essex
East Anglian Freight Terminal Ltd., Felixstowe
Erith Inland Clearance Depot, Erith, Kent
Glasgow Inland Rail Depot, Salkeld Street, Glasgow
Greenford Inland Clearance Depot, Greenford, Middlesex
Hull Euroscan Ltd., Dairycoates, Hull
Leeds Containerbase, Stourton, Leeds
Speke Freight Terminal, Liverpool
Liverpool Container Base (Bootle)
London (East) Inland Clearance Depot, Chobham Farm, Leyton Road, London E15
London (Stratford) International Freight, London E15
Lenham Inland Clearance Depot, Lenham, Nr. Maidstone
Manchester Containerbase, Urmston, Lancs
Manchester International Freight Terminal, Trafford Park
Milton Inland Clearance Depot, Milton Trading Estate, Abbingdon, Berks
Northampton Inland Clearance Depot, Round Spinney, Northampton

How to Export

Paddock Wood Inland Clearance Depot, Tonbridge, Kent
Sheepy Park Depot, Renfrew
Sutton International Freight Terminal, Sutton-in-Ashfield, Notts.

Free zones

Belfast Airport Free Zone
Birmingham Airport Free Zone
Cardiff Free Zone
Liverpool Free Zone
Prestwick Airport Free Zone
Southampton Free Zone

Appendix VII

World currencies

A

Abu Dhabi	UAE Dirham
Afghanistan	Afghani
Ajman	UAE Dirham
Aland Islands	Finnish Markka
Alaska	US Dollar
Albania	Lek
Algeria	Algerian Dinar
American Samoa	US Dollar
Andorra	Spanish Peseta
	French Franc
Angola (including Cabinda)	Kwanza
Anguilla	East Caribbean Dollar
Antigua and Barbuda	East Caribbean Dollar
Argentina	Argentinian Peso
Aruba	Dutch Antilles Guilder
Ascension	St Helena Pound
Australia	Australian Dollar
Australian Antarctic Territory	Australian Dollar
Australian Oceania: (Cocos (Keeling) Islands; Christmas Island (Indian Ocean); Heard and McDonald Islands; Norfolk Island)	Australian Dollar

Austria (excluding Jungholz and Mittelberg) — Schilling
Azores — Portuguese Escudo

B

Bahamas — Bahamian Dollar
Bahrain — Bahrani Dinar
Baker Island — US Dollar
Bangladesh (formerly East Pakistan) — Taka
Barbados — Barbadian Dollar
Belgium — Belgian Franc
Belize (formerly British Honduras) — Belize Dollar
Benin (formerly Dahomey) — West African Franc
Bermuda — Bermudan Dollar
Bhutan — Indian Rupee
Bolivia — Bolivian Peso
Bonaire — Dutch Antilles Guilder
Botswana — Pula
Brazil — Cruzero
British Antarctic Territory — Pound Sterling
British Indian Ocean Territory — Mauritius Rupee / Seychelles Rupee
British Virgin Islands — US Dollar
Brunei — Brunei Dollar
Bulgaria — Lev
Burkina Faso (formerly Upper Volta) — West African Franc
Burma — Kyat
Burundi — Burundese Franc

C

Cameroon — CFA Franc
Canada — Canadian Dollar
Canary Islands — Spanish Peseta
Cape Verde — Cape Verde Escudo
Caroline Islands — US Dollar
Cayman Islands — Cayman Island Dollar

Appendix VII

Central African. Republic	CFA Franc
Ceuta and Melilla (including Penon de Velez de la Gomera, Penon de Alhucemas and the Chafarinas Islands)	Spanish Peseta
Chad	CFA Franc
Chile	Chilean Peso
China	Yuan (Ren Min Bi)
Christmas Island (Indian Ocean)	Australian Dollar
Cocos Islands	Australian Dollar
Colombia	Colombian Peso
Comoros (Great Comoro Anjouan And Moheli)	Comoros Franc
Congo	CFA Franc
Continental Shelf NW European):	
Belgian Sector	Belgian Franc
Danish Sector	Danish Krone
French Sector	French Franc
German Sector	Deutsche Mark
Irish Sector	Punt
Netherlands Sector	Dutch Guilder
Norwegian Sector	Norwegian Krone
United Kingdom Sector	Pound Sterling
Cook Islands	New Zealand Dollar
Corn Islands	US Dollar
Costa Rica	Costa Rica Colon
Cuba	Cuban Peso
Curaçao	Dutch Antilles Guilder
Cyprus	Cypriot Pound
Czechoslovakia	Koruna

D

Denmark	Danish Krone
Desirade	French Franc
Djibouti	Djibouti Franc

Dominica	East Caribbean Dollar
Dominican Republic	Dominican Republic Peso
Dubai	UAE Dirham

E

Ecuador (including Galapagos Islands)	Sucre
Egypt	Egyptian Pound
El Salvador	El Salvador Colon
Equatorial Guinea (comprising Fernando Po and adjacent islets, Annobon, Corisco and the Elobey Islands (with adjacent islets) and Rio Muni)	Ekwele
Ethiopia	Bir
European Community	European Currency Unit

F

Falkland Islands	Falkland Island Pound
Faroe Islands	Danish Krone
Fiji	Fiji Dollar
Finland	Markka
France	French Franc
French Antarctic Territory	French Franc
French Guiana	French Franc
French Polynesia	CFP Franc
French Southern Territory	French Franc
Fujairah	UAE Dirham

G

Gabon	CFA Franc
Gambia	Dalasi
German Democratic Republic and East Berlin	East German Mark (Ostmark)

Appendix VII

Germany, Federal Republic of (including West Berlin, Jungholz and Mittelberg: excluding Busingen)	West German Mark (Deutsche Mark)
Ghana	Cedi
Gibraltar	Gibraltar Pound
Gough	St Helena Pound
Greece	Drachma
Greenland	Danish Krone
Grenada	East Caribbean Dollar
Guadeloupe	French Franc
Guam	US Dollar
Guatemala	Quetzal
Guernsey	Pound Sterling
Guinea	Syli
Guinea-Bissau (formerly Portuguese Guinea)	Guinea Peso
Guyana	Guyana Dollar

H

Haiti	Gourde
	US Dollar
Hawaii	US Dollar
Heard and McDonald Islands	Australian Dollar
Honduras	Lempira
Hong Kong	Hong Kong Dollar
Howland Islands	US Dollar
Hungary	Forint

I

Iceland	Icelandic Krona
Iles des Saintes	French Franc
India	Indian Rupee
Indonesia	Rupiah
Iran	Iranian Rial
Iraq	Iraqi Dinar
Irish Republic	Punt
Israel	Shekel
Italy	Lira
Ivory Coast	West African Franc

J

Jamaica	Jamaican Dollar
Jarvis Islands	US Dollar
Japan	Yen
Jersey	Pound Sterling
Johnston Islands	US Dollar
Jordan	Jordanian Dinar

K

Kampuchea (Cambodia)	Khmer Rial
Keeling Islands (Cocos)	Australian Dollar
Kenya	Kenya Shilling
Kingman Reef	US Dollar
Kiribati	Australian Dollar
Korea, North	Won
Korea, South	Won
Kuwait	Kuwaiti Dinar

L

Laos	Kip
Lebanon	Lebanese Pound
Lesotho	Malot
Liberia	Liberian Dollar
Libya	Libyan Dinar
Liechtenstein	Swiss Franc
Luxembourg	Luxembourg Franc

M

Macao	Pataca
Madagascar (Malgasy Republic)	Malgache Franc
Madeira	Portuguese Escudo
Malawi	Kwacha
Malaya	Ringgit
Maldives	Maldive Rupee
Mali	Mali Franc
Malta (including Gozo and Comino)	Maltese Pound
Man, Isle of (excluding ACP 80 transhipments to IOM Freeport)	Pound Sterling

Appendix VII

Man, Isle of (ACP 80 transhipments to IOM Freeport only)	Pound Sterling
Mariana Islands	US Dollars
Maria-Galante	French Franc
Marshall Islands	US Dollar
Martinique	French Franc
Mauritania	Ouguiya
Mauritius	Mauritius Rupee
Mayotte (Grand Terre and Pamanzi)	Comoros Franc
Mexico	Metical
Midway Island	US Dollar
Monaco	French Franc
Mongolia	Tugrik
Montserrat	East Caribbean Dollar
Morocco	Moroccan Dirham
Mozambique	Mozambique Metical

N

Nauru	Australian Dollar
Nepal	Nepalese Rupee
Netherlands	Dutch Guilder
New Caledonia Dependencies	CFP Franc
New Zealand	New Zealand Dollar
Niue	New Zealand Dollar
Nicaragua	Cordoba
Niger	W A Franc
Nigeria	Naira
Norfolk Island	Australian Dollar
Norway (Svalbard, including Spitsbergen, and Jan Mayen)	Norwegian Krone

O

Occupied Territories (West Bank of the Jordan and Gaza Strip)	Shelsel

Oman (formerly Muscan and Oman) — Omani Rial

P
Pakistan — Pakistani Rupee
Palmyra Island — US Dollar
Panama (including the former Canal Zone) — Balboa
Papua New Guinea — Kina
Paraguay — Guarani
Peru — Sol
Philippines — Philippine Peso
Pitcairn Island — New Zealand Dollar
Poland — Zloty
Polar Regions (not elsewhere specified) — Norwegian Krone
Portugal — Portuguese Escudo
Puerto Rico — US Dollar

Q
Qatar — Qatar Rial

R
Ras al Khaimah — UAE Dirham
Reunion — French Franc
Romania — Leu
Ross Dependency — New Zealand Dollar
Rwanda — Rwanda Franc

S
Saba — Dutch Antilles Guilder
Sabah — Ringgit
St Berthelemy — French Franc
St Christopher and Nevis, Federation of (St. Christopher may be referred to as St Kitts) — East Caribbean Dollar
St Eustatius — Dutch Antilles Guilder
St Helena — St Helena Pound
St Lucia — East Caribbean Dollar
St Maarten (South) — Dutch Antilles Guilder

Appendix VII

St Martin (North)	French Franc
St Pierre and Miquelon	French Franc
St Vincent	East Caribbean Dollar
San Marino	Lira
Sao Tome and Principe	Dobra
Sarawak	Ringgit
Saudi Arabia	Saudi Riyal
Senegal	West African Franc
Seychelles	Seychelles Rupee
Sharjah	UAE Dirham
Sierra Leone	Leone
Singapore	Singapore Dollar
Solomon Islands	Solomon Islands Dollar
Somalia	Somalia Shilling
South Africa	Rand
South West Africa (Namibia)	South African Rand
Soviet Union	Rouble
Spain (including Balearic Islands)	Spanish Peseta
Sri Lanka (formerly Ceylon)	Sri Lanka Rupee
Sudan	Sudanese Pound
Surinam	Surinam Guilder
Swan Islands	US Dollar
Swaziland (Ngwame)	Lilangeni
Sweden	Kron
Switzerland (including Liechtenstein, Busingen and Campione)	Swiss Franc
Syria	Syrian Pound

T

Taiwan	New Taiwan Dollar
Tanzania (Tanganyika, Zanzibar, Pemba)	Tanzania Shilling
Thailand	Baht
Togo	West African Franc
Tokelau Islands	New Zealand Dollar
Tonga	Pa'anga
Trinidad and Tobago	Trinidad and Tobago Dollar

How to Export

Tristan da Cunha	St Helena Dollar
Tunisia	Tunisian Dinar
Turkey	Turkish Lira
Turks and Caicos Islands	US Dollar
Tuvalu	Australian Dollar

U

Uganda	Ugandan Shilling
Umm al Qaiwain	UAE Dirham
United Kingdom (Great Britain), Northern Ireland and Isle of Man (excluding ACP80 transhipments to IOM Freeport)	Pound Sterling
United States Oceania	US Dollar
United States of America	US Dollar
Uruguay	Uruguay Peso
Uruguay Peso	

V

Vanuatu	Vanuatu Franc
Vatican City	Lira
Venezuela	Bolivar
Viet-Nam	Dong
Virgin Islands of USA	US Dollar

W

Wake Island	US Dollar
Wallis and Futuna Islands	CF Franc
Western Samoa	Tala

Y

Yemen, North	Yemeni Rial
Yemen, South	Yemeni Dinar
Yugoslavia	Yugoslavian Dinar

Appendix VII

Z

Zaire (formerly Congo Kinshasa)	Zaire
Zambia	Kwacha
Zimbabwe	Zimbabwean Dollar

Index

Advance Payment
  Guarantee, 58
Advertising, 25, 47
Advice and information, 15, 17-18, 19-20
Agents, 23, 24, 25, 35-6, 47, 48-9, 51
  agency agreement, 49-50
  appointment, 35, 47, 49
  commission, 23
  contracts, 35
  foreign legislation, 49
Air transport, 78-9
  Air Waybill (AWB), 61, 79, 102
  charter, 78, 79
  consolidations, 78, 79
  direct airline bookings, 78-9
  Warsaw Convention, 74
Arbitration, 36

Banks, 15, 18, 20, 33, 45, 53-4, 69
  arranging finance, 68
  banker's reference, 34
  foreign currency payments, 33
Bills of Exchange, 58, 63, 64-5, 105
  avalised, 30, 33
Bills of Lading, 35, 61, 64, 74, 75, 83, 100
  House, 101
Blacklist Certificates, 62-3
British Overseas Trade Board (BOTB), 15, 18, 19-20, 24, 45, 53, 88
  Area Advisory Groups, 20
  Export Intelligence Service (EIS), 18
  Export Marketing Research Scheme, 21, 24
  Export Representative Service, 49
  Help for Exporters, 53
  Hints to Exporters, 19, 51
British Standards Institution, 54, 130
  Technical Help for Exporters (THE), 25

Carriage of Goods by Road Act (1965), 74
Carriage of Goods by Sea Act (1971), 74
Cash Before Delivery (CBD), 22, 33
Cash On Delivery (COD), 22, 33, 52
Certificate of Origin, 107

153

Chambers of Commerce,
  15, 18, 19-20, 26, 32, 35,
  49, 53, 88
  ATA Carnets, 53
  foreign, 54
  International (ICC), 64,
    83
  letters of introduction, 53
  overseas offices, 36
  trade missions, 51
Channel Tunnel, 81
Combiterms, 77
Communications, 36-7, 52-3
Competition, researching,
  19, 125
Computer information
  systems, 27
Conditions of sale, 36
Confirming houses, 48
Consulates, 20, 36, 49
  Consular Invoices, 62
Contract,
  forward exchange, 44
  of Sale, 60-1,
Cost, Insurance, Freight
  (CIF) terms, 71-2, 73,
  127
Cost & Freight (C&F)
  terms, 72, 73, 127
Costs,
  manufacturing, 14
  marketing, 14
  packing, 77, 78
  pricing, 15, 18, 23, 126
  shipping, 14
  staff, 14
  storage, 78
  transport, 78
Council for Mutual
  Economic Assistance
  (COMECON), 42
Credit,
  Documentary Letter of,
    30, 31, 33, 35, 45, 58,
    59-64
  insurance, 27, 30, 34, 37,
    43

rating, 26-7, 30, 34
rating agency, 34
Revolving, 60
Standby, 60
Term Bill, 64
Transferable, 60
Cultural differences, 41
Customer,
  banker's reference, 34
  credit status, 26-7, 30, 34

Delivery,
  late, 78
  terms, 34
Demurrage charges, 64
Direct mailing, 22, 47
Discounting bills, 30
Distribution trends, 19
Distributors, 47, 48-9, 51
  appointment, 47
  contracts, 35
  foreign legislation, 49
Documentary Collection,
  58, 64-5
Documentary Letter of
  Credit, 45, 58, 59-64, 68,
    87, 88, 106
  Contract of Sale, 60-1
  Cost, Insurance, Freight,
    (CIF), 71-2
  documentation, 61-3
  insurance clause, 71
  international rules, 64, 83
  Irrevocable, 59-60
  Irrevocable Confirmed,
    30, 33, 45, 58, 59, 60,
    72
  Revocable, 59
  shipment dates, 31, 35
Documentation, 31-2, 34-5,
  68, 85-90, 94
  Air Waybill, 61, 79, 102
  Bill of Lading, 35, 61,
    64, 74, 75, 83, 100, 101
  Certificate of Insurance,
    104

Index

Certificate of Origin, 107
CIM note, 81
CMR note, 81, 103
Documentary Letters of Credit, 61-3
Documents of Title, 64
EUR 1 Movement Certificate, 87, 109
export administration company, 86, 125
export cargo shipping instructions, 87
export invoice, 86-7, 98
export starter kit, 86
insurance certificates, 62
invoices, 36, 61-2
Postal Customs Declaration, 108
Postal Despatch note, 108
report of findings, 62, 88
shipping instruction note, 99
Single Administrative Document (SAD), 86, 88-90, 110-23

Embassies, 20, 36, 49
  foreign, 54
EUR 1 Movement Certificate, 87
European Community (EEC), 42
  Customs Carnet, 53
  differing VAT rates, 18, 24
  Lome agreement, 19
  Single Administrative Document (SAD), 88-90
Exchange restrictions, 18
Exhibitions, 21
Export administration companies, 86, 125
Export Credits Guarantee Department (ECGD), 27, 34, 43, 45

Export Merchants, 47

Factoring, 30
FBL, 83
Finance, 68-9
  aid funds, 19
  credit insurance, 27, 30, 34, 37, 43
  payment *see* Payment
  status reports and credit ratings, 26-7, 30, 34
  venture capital companies, 32
Foreign currency, 26
  accounts, 44, 66
  borrowing, 44-5, 67-8
  exchange-rate fluctuations, 33, 66, 126
  foreign exchange exposure, 44
  forward exchange contracts, 44, 66-7
  forward selling, 33
  invoicing in, 43-4
  option contract, 67
  payment in, 30, 33, 43-5, 66-8, 69
Forfaiting capital goods, 30
Forward exchange contract, 44, 66-7
Free on Board (FOB) terms, 72, 73, 77, 128
Freight forwarders, 22, 31, 34, 81, 83, 84, 86, 88, 125
  House Airway Bill (HAWB) 79

Geographic considerations, 40

Hague Visby Rules, 74
Handling charges, 23
High commissions, 20, 49

Import restrictions, 18, 41-3, 50

155

Incoterms, 77
Institute of Export, 20, 27, 32, 35
   training courses, 32, 25
Instructions, translation, 25
Insurance, 126
   buyer fails to insure, 72
   cargo, 27, 34, 71-6
   carrier's liabilities, 73-5
   certificate of, 62, 104
   Cost, Insurance, Freight (CIF), 71-2
   costs, 23
   credit, 27, 30, 34, 37, 43
   currency fluctuations, 126
   goods damaged in transit, 72, 91-2
   making a claim, 75-6
   Sellers' Interest Contingency cover, 72
Interest charges, 23
International Court of Arbitration (ICC), 36
Invoices, 61-2
   Consular, 62
   export, 86-7, 98
   in foreign currencies, 43-4
   selling conditions, 36

Know-how as export, 15

Labelling product, 31
Language, 41, 95-6
   product instructions, 25-6, 31
   skills, 14, 31
   telephone communications, 52
Letter of Credit *see* Documentary Letter of Credit
Letters of Introduction, 53
Local manufacturing base, setting up, 43, 47, 50
Local market requirements, 25

London Court of International Arbitration, 36

Market research, 18-21, 40
   British Overseas Trade Board, 21
   checklist, 125
   delivery methods, 36
   desk research, 19
   distribution trends, 19
   establishing demand, 17
   field visits, 19, 21, 24, 30, 36, 47
   market's growth pattern, 19
   nature of competition, 19
   packaging, 36
   storage methods, 36
   trade fairs, 21
Market-led companies, 30
Marketing costs, 14

Non-tariff barriers, 18, 41
Orders,
   checklist, 126
   unsolicited, 45

Packing and packaging, 14, 34
   climatic conditions, 26, 91-2
   costs, 23, 77, 78
   design, 25
   export packing companies, 31
   market research, 36
   transport methods, 26, 77
Paper and Board, Printing and Packaging Industries Research Association (PIRA), 26
Payment, 43-6, 57-69
   in advance, 58
   Advance Payment Guarantee, 58

Index

bad debt avoidance, 45-6
barter, 58
Bills of Exchange, 30, 33, 58, 63, 64-5, 105
Cash Before Delivery (CBD), 22, 33
Cash On Delivery (COD), 22, 33, 52
countertrade, 58
credit insurance, 27, 30, 34, 37, 43
debt factoring, 30
debt-chasing systems, 37
discounting bills, 30
Documentary Collection (Bills of Exchange), 58, 64-5
Documentary Letter of Credit, 30, 31, 33, 35, 45, 58, 59-64, 68, 71, 72, 87, 88, 106
 in foreign currency, 33, 43-5, 66-8, 69
 forfaiting, 30
 open accounts, 37, 58, 65-6
 Revolving Credit, 60
 Standby Credit, 60
 status reports and credit ratings, 26-7, 30, 34
 Term Bill, 64
 terms, 32-4
 Transferable Credits, 60
Pricing, 15, 23-4, 126
 unprofitable levels, 18
Product, adaptability, 14
 capital goods, 30
 costing, 15
 despatch, 34-5
 pricing, 15, 18, 23-4, 126
 promotion, 25-6, 30
Production,
 administration, 34-5
 assessing facilities, 31
 component supply, 31
 excess capacity, 14

scheduling, 31

Quotation, 125

Rail transport, 81
 CIM note, 81
 freight forwarders, 81
Report of Findings, 62, 88
Revolving Credit, 60
Road transport, 79-81
 CMR note, 81, 103
 Freight-All-Kinds (FAK) basis, 80
Royalty fees, limited, 50

Sales and marketing, 35-6, 47-50
 associate company, 47
 commission agents, 48
 confirming houses, 48
 export merchants, 47, 48
 field visits, 47, 48, 50, 51-2
 local agents and distributors, 47
 local manufacturing base, 43, 47, 50
 overseas sales office, 47, 50, 51
 sales personnel, 37, 47, 48
 subsidiary company, 47
Sea transport, 81-4
 Bills of Lading, 35, 61, 64, 74, 75, 83, 100, 101
 Bunker Adjustment Factor (BAF), 82
 Conference lines, 82
 Currency Adjustment Factor (CAF), 82
 freight forwarders, 83
 Freight-All-Kinds (FAK) basis, 83
 Full Container Load (FCL), 82
 Hague Visby Rules, 74

Less-than-Container Load (LCL) (groupage), 83
non-Conference lines, 82
roll on/roll off (ro/ro), 79
Standard Shipping Note, 83
Selection of export market, 39-46
Services as export, 15
Shipping instruction note, 99
Simplification of International Trade Procedures Board (SITPRO), 86
Single Administrative Document (SAD), 86, 88-90, 110-23
Staff,
　costs, 14
　language skills, 14, 31, 41
　training, 32
Standby Credit, 60
Statistics and Market Intelligence Library (SMIL), 17, 19
Stoppage in transitu, 72
Storage methods, 36

Tariff barriers, 41-3
Taxation and duties, 23, 41
　Carnets, 53
　Postal Customs Declaration, 108
　Value Added Tax, 18, 24
　withholding taxes, 50
Technical requirements, differing, 24, 25, 54
Tender offers,
　selling conditions, 36
Term Bill, 64
Trade,
　barriers, 18, 41-3, 50
　blocs, 41-3
　fairs, 21, 30

missions, 24, 51
Trade Associations, 17-18, 19-20
export committees, 17-18
trade missions, 51
Transferable Credits, 60
Transport, 14, 34, 36, 77-84, 125, 126
air, 61, 74, 78-9
Air Waybill, 61, 79, 102
airfreight, 64
Bills of Lading, 35, 61, 64, 74, 75, 83, 100, 101
cargo insurance, 27, 34, 71-6
carrier's liabilities, 73-5
CMR Convention Conditions, 74, 81
costs, 14, 23, 34, 78
demurrage charges, 64
documentation, 61, 64
export cargo shipping instructions, 87
freight forwarders, 22, 31, 34, 79, 81, 84, 86, 88, 125
goods damaged in transit, 72, 91-2
Hague Visby Rules, 74
late delivery penalties, 78
package design, 26
parcel post, 64
Post Office, 22, 33, 108
rail, 81
road, 79-81
sea, 79, 81-4
stoppage in transitu, 72
time factor, 78
Warsaw Convention, 74
Travel,
　advice, 54
　Green Card, 54
　International Driving Licence, 54

Value Added Tax (VAT), 18, 24

Index

Venture capital companies, 32

Warsaw Convention, 74

Withholding taxes, 50
World Bank aid fund, 19